ISBN 978-88-8398-095-4

Florence, Italy
www.e-p-a-p.com
www.europeanpress.eu

The European Parliament Administration facing the challenge of eDemocracy

Giancarlo Vilella

European Press Academic Publishing

Florence, Italy

On the cover: Image by Thomas Schwarz from Pixabay

Table of Contents

Scope

This book tries to offer a *complete analytical and operational paper, in view of the development of the European Parliament Administration (EPA) on the issue of e-Democracy.* As the European Parliament Secretary General, Klaus Welle, stated: "*The impact of technology on the functioning of democracy is nowadays very strong and is causing profound changes: this concerns the way of working of MEPs but above all of the administration. EPA is since years dealing with digital transformation and innovation: what we need now is defining a clear journey for facing the challenges of eDemocracy by shaping a multisector approach*". This study is a consequence of the request of the EP Secretary General; it takes into account what is already under way, together with the possible developments[1].

The study begins by taking into account the analysis contained in the reflection paper "*Working methods of the European Parliament Administration*[2]": Chapter 3 and the Conclusions of that paper analyse the topic of eDemocracy, setting out the following ideas. First of all: the concept of eDemocracy is evolving in a contradictory manner. There are those who argue that digital democracy is replacing democracy as we know it today, especially representative democracy. Or, on the contrary (as I believe), it is contended that eDemocracy must

[1]The official report (final version) has been submitted to the Secretary General in November 2020 and discussed in an internal seminar on 11 December 2020 in Brussels.

[2]The paper was the result of my fellowship at European University Institute in Florence (2018-19): it became a book under the title *Working methods of the European Parliament Administration in Multi-actors World. A case study*, European Press Academic Publishing, Florence, 2019.

be seen as an evolution of representative democracy in the sense of the expansion of its borders and, therefore, in the sense of its strengthening: in this context there are more and more occasions when the term "augmented democracy" is used, it being apparently more inclusive than the term eDemocracy. It is evident anyway that technology is:

- changing the way MEPs communicate with citizens
- creating a permanent connection that enables greater information sharing
- allowing greater participation in the democratic process
- allowing MEP's local offices in their constituencies to increase mobility and flexibility
- an excellent tool for making public action more transparent and promoting public participation
- an excellent tool for reinforcing the work of Parliament or any other political body.

Secondly it means that the administration must adapt to the new reality (by providing the best, modern services to empower its activities). In our daily role as public managers, we need to have a better knowledge of just how the world around us is changing through technology in order to understand, and steer the digital transformation of the administration of the European Parliament. Every innovation in the political and administrative spheres is now very dependent on technology; we must understand the context in which this is happening.

Third, the EU is committed to the achievement, defence and promotion of democracy as a fundamental value as the EU Treaty makes clear: Article 2[3], Articles 3 and 13 (which guarantee the protection of our fundamental values both within the Union and vis-à-vis third countries), Article 7 (which provides for a procedure against Member States which attack these essential values) and Article 49 (which requires respect for essential values as a condition for EU membership)[4].

[3]Article 2 TEU: *The Union is founded on the values of respect for human dignity, freedom, democracy, equality, the rule of law and respect for human rights, including the rights of persons belonging to minorities. These values are common to the Member States in a society in which pluralism, nondiscrimination, tolerance, justice, solidarity and equality between women and men prevail.*

[4]For an in-depth analysis, see: EPRS, *Protecting the rule of law in the EU. Ex-*

By these means, democracy defends itself at supranational level. But the defence of democracy cannot be static, by which I mean that an immobile, immutable system cannot be defended. Democracy defends itself by evolving and enlarging its conceptual boundaries, which is facilitated by the appropriation of technology as a normal working tool. Transparency, access to documents, consultation and dialogue, inclusion of citizens and co-administration are so many tools which go to widen the boundaries of modern democracy: technology is essential to make these tools operational. In all this, the administration (that is to say, of civil servants and the administrative organisation) plays what is acknowledged to be a decisive role, thanks to the action and skills of the staff.

The contents of the study "*Working methods of the European Parliament Administration*" were discussed at several meetings in the months following their publication[5]. Each meeting devoted part of the debate to the issues relating to eDemocracy contained in the study and provided new food for thought for this report. However, Enrico Francesconi's observation during the EPRS Book Talk was particularly relevant[6]: he emphasised and analysed the link between European Democracy and eDemocracy, suggesting the concept of "connecting people" as a hinge between the two aspects so as to bring them together. In this respect, the work of the European Parliament's administration (EPA) is essential. Also during the Luxembourg meetings, the concept of eDemocracy was particularly prominent in the discussions: the idea that recurred frequently with a view to giving eDemocracy concrete form was that of "dialogue", which is the means of contact with citizens and of empathy between them and the political-institutional level. Here, too, the role of the administration

---

isting mechanisms and possible improvements, authored by R. Manko, November 2019, PE 642.280.

[5]I would mention especially: (a) the exchange of views with the EP Staff Committee plenary meeting in Strasbourg on 21 October 2019, (b) the EPAP presentation of the book in Luxembourg on 5 December 2019, (c) *Discussing Giancarlo Vilella's book*, Università degli Studi di Milano, Milan, 9 December 2019, (d) the EPRS Book Talk, *The EPA: strategy and working methods*, Brussels, 8 January 2020 and (e) Max Planck Institute, *Book Talk*, Luxembourg, 22 January 2020.

[6]EPRS Book Talk, cited in the preceding note.

becomes central in the management of dialogue.

In addition, it is very important to remind that the EP Administration has published a huge EPRS Study on eDemocracy in the European Union[7]: in the Study, the eDemocracy is linked with the innovative political approach, which supports e-participation, e-consultation, e-information, e-decision making. Those are all concepts on which we come back in developing the present report. Moreover, in a supplementary analysis on civic engagement, we read that "with online spaces having replaced physical spaces as venues for political argument and social interaction, the full digitalisation of democratic processes seems inevitable (...) unconventional forms of civic engagement are replacing offline, face-to-face forms of participation[8]". The same document stresses that "in general, bureaucracies have been slow to adapt to technological change[9]". Well: that is not the case with the EPA. The present report shows how advanced the EPA is in terms of both projects implemented and projects in progress when it comes to adaptation to eDemocracy.

Even more, while I was developing my analysis, the issue was brought to everyone's attention when the Coronavirus Covid-19 emergency broke out, as a result of which the search for solutions for the proper functioning of the institution required reflection on the use of technologies in such situations by safeguarding democracy. The issue will be dealt with in depth in Chapter 1 (on the impact of Covid-19 on the functioning of democracy), Chapter 6 (on the consequences for the protection of personal data) and the Conclusions (on the political and technological solutions adopted by the European Parliament to

[7]EPRS/STOA, *Prospects for e-democracy in Europe*, February 2018, PE 603.213, under the responsibility of G. Quaglio and T. Karapiperis, the Study has been prepared by several authors. The EPRS Study is divided into three phases: a) a literature review; b) an empirical assessment; c) and policy options.

[8]EPRS, *Digital democracy. Is the future of civic engagement online?*, authored by G. Sgueo, February 2020, PE 646.161.

[9]ibid. For a broad, in-depth examination of examples of participatory democracy with community civic engagement from various regions of the world, see EPRS, *The practice of democracy. A selection of civic engagement initiatives*, authored by G. Sgueo, June 2020, PE 651.970. The study focuses on taking inspiration from such initiatives in order to counteract political apathy and the decline in citizens' trust.

address the situation).

All these elements, together with the strong preference of the Secretary General, Klaus Welle for a European Parliament which is closest to citizens, and the clear preference of the President of Parliament, David Sassoli, for an EU "in which the people feel their voices are heard," mean[10] that the EPA should adopt a holistic approach to eDemocracy. We shall see how as this report develops.

Structure

Based on this starting point, the analysis set out in this report will be articulated as follows:

- Democracy in trouble: an introduction
- The political impulse of the Plenary
- Possible prospects
- The state of the art inside the EPA
- Operational proposal
- Critical remarks
- Conclusions and Closing.

Democracy in trouble (an introduction) takes into account the wide-ranging debate being conducted on the difficulties experienced by the democratic system: evidently, by this I mean not the democratic system as a whole, but some important aspects of it. That is to say, negative mechanisms within it, authoritarian aspirations, the influence of the economic crisis or of economic approaches, populism, emergency situation (i.e. Covid-19) and so on. This rapid survey of the challenges facing modern democracy is necessary in order to understand the context in which the emergence of eDemocracy is situated, bringing novelty, support and a new vision of things.

The political impulse of the Plenary: the pillar of this chapter is the European Parliament Resolution of 16 March 2017[11], where we read that "democracy should evolve and adapt to changes and opportunities related to new ICT technologies and tools", which reflects a

[10] They both mirror the opinion of EP, that's why they are so relevant.

[11] European Parliament resolution of 16 March 2017 on e-democracy in the European Union: potential and challenges, P8_TA(2017)095

clear awareness of a process of change which is under way. A number of specific tools are identified in this Resolution for developing eDemocracy (including e-government, e-participation, e-voting and many others). There are, however, several other resolutions adopted by the Plenary which mention the tools of eDemocracy and call for them to be implemented: the most significant of these are analysed below. Particular attention is paid to the resolution on the future of Europe, which is considered in the context of the debate on the election of the new European Commission and its priority policies.

The chapter on *Possible prospects* undertakes an in-depth analysis of the meaning of each of the digital tools singled out by the Plenary, from both the theoretical and the practical points of view. Taking those meanings into account, the possible effects on the structure of the European Parliament and its activities are also analysed.

The state of the art inside the EPA: the European Parliament became conscious of the importance of the phenomenon at a relatively early date. Indeed, Directorate-General ITEC for Innovation and Technological Support, was created in 2007 and endowed with substantial resources, which have been increased over time. Moreover, in the two studies, *The European Parliament 2025 – Preparing for complexity*[12], *and MEP 2025 – Preparing the Future Work Environment for Members of the European Parliament*[13], the question was examined in great detail in 2012: over the course of the following years, all the recommendations contained in the two documents inspired the internal policies for technological innovation. This chapter focuses on what has been set up within the institution and what is in progress: to this end, an in-depth analysis of the Strategic Execution Framework (SEF)/Parliamentary Project Portfolio (PPP) and DG ITEC's project has been carried out.

[12]The European Parliament 2025 – *Preparing for complexity*, Brussels, January 2012. https://www.europarl.europa.eu/RegData/etudes/STUD/2012/479851/SG_STUD(2012)479851_EN.pdf

[13]"MEP 2025": *Preparing the Future Work Environment for Members of the European Parliament* – Identifying Future Trends in Technology which may Impact on Society and therefore on EP work Structures and Processes, Brussels, March 2012. https://www.europarl.europa.eu/thinktank/en/document.html?reference=IPOL-JOIN_ET(2012)453231

The *Operational proposal* is simply a consequence of the preceding analysis in so far as it sets out to see what could or should still be done in the near future in order to support the development of eDemocracy and confront its challenges. There are many projects or ideas on the table: in particular, the documents prepared for the Innovation Day 2020, the DG ITEC Strategic orientations and the SEF 2019-21 are analysed.

In the chapter *Critical Remarks*, after reaffirming the definition of eDemocracy adopted by the Plenary and recalling the challenges of modern democracy, the analysis is completed by theoretical references to the risks for democracy arising from the spread of technology. The most important risks include disintermediation and the weakening of representation, the transformation of information into an economic commodity, asymmetric control over users, and the lack of rules on web operators. Hence the importance – as stressed in the chapter – of policies on the protection of personal data and IT security, on which the European Parliament has acted.

The *Conclusions* summarise the results of the study. There is a very high awareness on the part of the European Parliament in favour of eDemocracy, both at political level (official positions of the Plenary) and at the level of the administration. The EPA has, in fact, adopted solutions that prefigure a definable approach to eDemocracy. The report closes with the list of everything that has been done (included during the Covid-19 emergency) and everything that is planned, with the proposal not to add other projects to the ones already under way. The final suggestion is to structure the sector organisationally so as to make it uniform and with a multi-sector approach: the hypothesis submitted is to do it by means of a transversal Steering Working Group, coordinated at the level of the Secretary General's Cabinet, while making it a corporate goal.

The report focuses entirely on the work of the EPA, its projects and its organisation, but it goes without saying that the idea underlying the whole reflection is that the administration is first and foremost at the service of the activity of the Members and the fulfilment of the institution's tasks. It is to this end that the action of the EPA in general and of eDemocracy in particular must be directed.

One last caveat: throughout the report I use the term "technology" in an apparently neutral way: in reality what I am referring to essentially is "digital technology", except when something else is expressly indicated.

Chapter 1

Democracy in trouble: an introduction

Europe's aspiration to democracy and the will to make it ever better come down to us from antiquity: it has involved ongoing quest between (as they say) ups and downs, where for millennia the downs have been absolutely dominant right up to modern times. In the last two centuries, things have improved considerably, and even tragedies have been overcome, until we attained liberal democracy, the most advanced and mature level reached by the political organisation of society, a level where the two terms that make up the word, demos and cratia, take on their full meaning. Nevertheless, democracy has always been condemned as teetering on the verge of bankruptcy and people have been writing it off for decades: E. Fawcett[1] lists authoritative books from the 1930s to the present day that take this line.

The Covid-19 emergency, in addition, has even brought many analysts to the conclusion that the situation is a risk for democracy: for instance, the successful author Y. N. Harari says that "[t]he storm will pass, humankind will survive, most of us will still be alive – but we will inhabit a different world[2]". What world? It depends on the choices we make: "The first" – says Harari – "is between totalitarian

[1]E. Fawcett, *Liberalism. The Life of an Idea*, Princeton University Press, Oxford, 2019

[2]Y. N. Harari, *The world after coronavirus*, Financial Times, 20 March 2020.

surveillance and citizen empowerment"[3]. He is not alone in taking this view. Another example, among many, is the appeal made to the institutions by a group of intellectuals in Italy[4]: the appeal contends that "all at home" (confinement) is poisonous for the institutions because it puts democracy into quarantine. According to the authors of the appeal, Parliament assembles only intermittently, converts decrees into laws hastily and does not exercise its power of holding the executive to account; the government meets at night and communicates through social media; the Prime Minister limits constitutional rights by decree, and so on. Democracy cannot be suspended, the appeal says, because if "you resign yourself to something today, you will lose freedom tomorrow". In France, the debate was limited to the fact that Parliament's activity was so curtailed, owing to the restrictions, that it was regarded as an unprecedented event in French parliamentary history compared with other crises in the past[5]. The debate was useful and had effects: indeed, when in October 2020 France decided to re-impose a generalised confinement on account of the devastating new wave of the virus, the decisions of the executive and the President were submitted to a vote of the National Assembly and the Senate, after all parties had been consulted.

The question has also been raised in Belgium on account of the exceptional powers ("*pouvoirs spéciaux*") conferred on federal or regional executives: here too, the question is whether the guarantees of democratic control are ensured and remain sufficient if parliament (with the regional parliaments) continues to exercise its activities but with means and methods adapted to the situation[6]. In Belgium the most widespread phenomenon has in fact been legal proceedings brought against the State on account of the restrictive measures adopted: some lawyers consider that certain rules imposed because of the epidemic are contrary to the rule of law, such as the closure of commercial

[3]ibid. See also EPRS, *Covid-19's impact on human rights outside the EU*, authored by I. Zamfir, PE 649.365, April 2020.

[4]The first signatory was Prof. Marcello Pera, a former President of the Senate of the Italian Republic: see Corriere della Sera, 25 March 2020.

[5]Le Figaro, 1 April 2020

[6]See in particular the extensive inquiry of Bernard Demonty in Le Soir of 26 March 2020.

activities, the suspension of teaching, the tracking imposed on bars and restaurants, and so on. In October 2020 as many as 85 civil liability proceedings were pending before the Belgium Council of State. When the Council of State held that it was possible for the executive to take measures which restrict our freedoms to a considerable degree, the reaction of many constitutional lawyers was one of alarm and they called for intervention by means of legislative acts adopted by parliament in order to stave off any possible future drift in this direction[7].

But the case that has raised the greatest concerns, not to say denunciations of a drift towards authoritarianism, is that of Hungary. On the occasion of the Covid-19 emergency, the Hungarian Parliament granted Prime Minister Viktor Orbán sweeping powers not only to govern unsupervised, without checks and balances, but also to prolong the state of emergency indefinitely without the approval of Parliament. To this must be added the suspension of laws by decree and the introduction of a curfew and arrest for obstructing public efforts or spreading false information[8]. Some consider this a coup d'état and the beginning of a dictatorship, with Covid-19 as a mere pretext[9]. The European Parliament also weighed in on the rule of law in Hungary. *President Sassoli said after e-meeting the heads of the political groups that he'll write to the Commission to ask what it intends to do about Orbán's new über-powers, "and to assess whether this constitutes a serious violation of Article 2 of the EU Treaty ? which outlines our values, based on democracy and freedom." This is what a self-confident Parliament looks like: "Our message is clear: democracy continues to function," said Sassoli. "All parliamentary bodies are continuing to work to tackle the Covid-19 emergency. We have ensured that MEPs are still able to meet remotely, participate in*

---

[7]For all these events, see the reports in Le Soir of 29 October, 3 November and 6 November 2020.

[8]In fact, the consequences of the measures in Hungary were immediately apparent with the arrest of opponents of the government, accused of spreading "fake news" on social media. This gave rise to criticism and concern, but no concrete action to challenge the legality of the measures: Le Soir, 23-24 May 2020.

[9]Corriere della Sera, 31 March 2020; Le Soir, 31 March 2020; Le Figaro, 1 April 2020.

debates, propose amendments and vote." The next plenary, in mid-April, will deal with the corona crisis: "MEPs will discuss and debate, and we will update our position on how to deal with the catastrophe. Democracy will continue."[10] Indeed, verifying the proportionality of the measures taken and their compliance with fundamental rights and rule of law concerns all EU countries and it is the task of the European Commission to make an initial analysis and submit the results to the European Council.

The Commission is sometimes criticised for not being sufficiently active in this field, but this time its reaction was relatively swift. Commissioner Jourovà, who is responsible, among other things, for questions relating to the rule of law, made a statement saying that the Corona virus must be killed but democracy must survive. With regard to Hungary, the Commissioner specifically said: " *What raises the attention not only at the Commission but also of many other bodies is the context. What we hear from the Hungarian side is 'read the law'. Fair enough. We read the law... but the context is rather problematic because in Hungarian law we already saw the tendencies to concentrate the power," she added. "I think that Mr [Viktor] Orbán [the Hungarian prime minister] cannot be surprised that now he sees such a reaction ... I would say that Mr Orbán will have to prove that these concerns are unfounded."*[11] The European Parliament has intervened on this matter in a direct and determined manner at its highest political level, since the plenary adopted a resolution[12] devoting a whole section (paras 46-55) to the protection of democracy, the rule of law and fundamental rights. In this section, Parliament also discusses internal border controls, reception of new asylum seekers, health tracking, disinformation and the financial difficulties experienced by the media,

---

[10] The passage in italics is taken word for word from the report in the POLITICO Brussels Playbook of 3 April 2020; however if you wish to hear the whole of President Sassoli's statement, you should access to: https://multimedia.europarl.europa.eu/en/statement-sassoli-following-meeting-conference-presidents_I187872

[11] For this declaration and other more extensive and more detailed statements, see POLITICO Brussels Playbook, 10 April 2020.

[12] European Parliament resolution of 17 April 2020 on EU coordinated action to combat the COVID-19 pandemic and its consequences, P9_TA PROV(2020)0054

and sexual and reproductive rights. But the first two paragraphs are directly concerned with the problems of the functioning of democracy, stating as follows:

- *Underlines that the Charter of Fundamental Rights of the European Union and compliance with the rule of law must continue to apply, and that in the context of emergency measures, the authorities must ensure that everyone enjoys the same rights and protection; emphasises that all measures taken at national and/or EU level must be in line with the rule of law, strictly proportionate to the exigencies of the situation, clearly related to the ongoing health crisis, limited in time and subjected to regular scrutiny; deems it totally incompatible with European values both the decision from the Hungarian Government to prolong the state of emergency indefinitely, to authorise the Government to rule by decree without time limit, and to weaken the emergency oversight of the Parliament, and the steps taken by the Polish Government*
- *namely changing the electoral code against the judgment of Constitutional Tribunal and provisions laid by law – to hold Presidential elections in the middle of a pandemic, which may endanger the lives of Polish citizens and undermine the concept of free, equal, direct and secret elections as enshrined in the Polish Constitution;*
- *Calls, therefore, on the Commission to urgently assess whether the emergency measures are in conformity with the Treaties and to make full use of all available EU tools and sanctions to address this serious and persistent breach, including budgetary ones, underlining once again the imminent need for an EU mechanism on democracy, the rule of law and fundamental rights; urges the Council to put back on its agenda the discussions and procedures related to the ongoing Article 7 procedures*[13].

[13]ibid., paras 46-47; Yet, despite all these pressures and concerns, it would seem (at the time of writing) that the European Commission has no intention to meddle, because after a thorough and detailed analysis of "the text itself" it sees no reason to intervene: as reported by POLITICO, Brussels Playbook of 30 April 2020.

At the European Council level, some Member States also took the initiative to make a declaration in defence of democracy, even in exceptional circumstances. It reads as follows: "*In this unprecedented situation, it is legitimate that Member States adopt extraordinary measures to protect their citizens and overcome the crisis. We are however deeply concerned about the risk of violations of the principles of rule of law, democracy and fundamental rights arising from the adoption of certain emergency measures. Emergency measures should be limited to what is strictly necessary, should be proportionate and temporary in nature, subject to regular scrutiny, and respect the aforementioned principles and international law obligations. They should not restrict the freedom of expression or the freedom of the press. We need to jointly overcome this crisis and to jointly uphold our European principles and values on this path. We therefore support the European Commission initiative to monitor the emergency measures and their application to ensure the fundamental values of the Union are upheld, and invite the General Affairs Council to take up the matter when appropriate.*"[14]

In short, also an emergency (in this case a health emergency, but we have also experienced a terrorism emergency or immigration emergency) is a factor which puts democracy at risk, included its representative institutions such as parliaments[15]: this is the reason why

---

[14] *Diplomatic statement / 01-04-2020. Statement by Belgium, Denmark, Estonia, Finland, France, Germany, Greece, Ireland, Italy, Latvia, Lithuania, Luxembourg, the Netherlands, Portugal, Spain, Sweden.* See: https://www.government.nl/documents/diplomatic-statements/2020/04/01/statement-by-belgium-denmark-finland-france-germany-greece-ireland-italy-luxembourg-the-netherlands-portugal-spain-sweden

[15] On the practical response to Covid-19 emergency by the Parliaments around the world see IPU-Centre for Innovation in Parliament, *Parliamentary Responses to Coronavirus*, Live Document, Technical Update of April 2020. Another very interesting document has been prepared by the Commonwealth Parliamentary Association, *Covid-19. Delivering Parliamentary Democracy*, London, April 2020, where the problems arising from the health emergency are analysed in depth, including lack of scrutiny, lack of expertise or access to experts, too much Executive Power, and increased pressure. The document offers suggestions for policy actions to be taken, but stresses the need to find technological solutions for the functioning of the institution. Last, as far as the EU Member States' Parliaments are concerned see the excellent synthesis developed in EPRS, *Parliaments in emer-*

there is general agreement on the need to set strict time limits to special powers in emergency situations, such as that of Covid-19, in democratic countries, where, moreover, there it must be obligatory to justify them.

Recently, concerns (of a varying degree of sincerity) about the fate of democracy have multiplied, so much so that it is impossible to keep track of it all. But among the most interesting, we can certainly mention the work by D. Runciman[16], who essentially maintains that today there are events and mechanisms that erode democracies from within: "electoral fraud, limitations on the rule of law, personal powers of the executive leader" and so on. This is then aggravated by the casual and incorrectly generalised use of concepts such as "coup d'état", "coup", "crisis": in this way real phenomena and their development are no longer understood. According to Runciman, there are two trends (among many) undermining the nature of modern democracy: on the one hand, the fact that there is no longer any comparison made between different but reasoned opinions, but rather a clash of alternative worlds; on the other, there is the fact that leaders do not aim to galvanise the population in a positive and constructive direction, but to excite anger and frustration. The author concludes that with this erosion we are moving toward illiberal democracies that will ultimately give way to forms of authoritarianism, like the developed and insidious authoritarianism seen in China. N. Baverez[17] stresses that "indisputably the most serious danger to democracies comes from within: from the time of Athens until the 1930s there have been few cases in which democracies fell because they were defeated from outside". Today, according to the author, the most serious mistake of democracies has been to underestimate the populists, who were regarded as lacking in seriousness and false and therefore irrelevant, whereas they already had a clear project in mind against the independence of the judiciary, the media, the universities and against the system of checks and balances in general.

---

gency mode How Member States' parliaments are continuing with business during the pandemic, authored by M. Díaz Crego and R. Mańko, PE 649.396, April 2020.

[16]D. Runciman, *How Democracy Fails*, Profile Books, London, 2018.

[17]N. Baverez, *L'alerte démocratique*, L'Observatoire, Paris, 2020.

S. Levitsky and D. Ziblatt[18] also go in the same direction, while deepening the analysis on the attitude of leaders with authoritarian aspirations: rejection of the rules of the democratic game, tolerance of violence, the will to restrict the civil liberties of opponents and denial of the legitimacy of the opposition. In particular, leaders with authoritarian tendencies claim for themselves the moral monopoly over representing their people. During the 1950s, G. Sartori[19] had already intuited that liberal democracy would be put under pressure and overcome by the emergence of an illiberal democracy, defined by him as "aliberal" and also totalitarian. Democracy, Sartori said, would remain as an empty shell, nominal only and destined to disappear definitively

Another kind of critical analysis focuses instead on the economic aspects. The last ten to fifteen years (in particular 2007-2017) have been characterised by a global economic and social crisis, which is also a crisis of international relations: the difficulties of the crisis have been widened, even more so by the perception of the explosion of migratory flows that reached unprecedented levels in 2015 and 2016. Effective responses were provided to this crisis, above all at the supranational level, but the reaction has been largely negative because, rather than considering the reality of things (the complexity of problems, the protections and the actual bailouts), it was based on abstract expectations.

There is a great contradiction of our time to which attention has been clearly drawn: according to Kershaw, we in Europe live in the most prosperous, free and peaceful era in all our history and yet there is a strong, widespread feeling of insecurity[20]. Kershaw argues that, apart from terrorist atrocities, the main reasons for this insecurity consist of uncertainty about our ability to cope with a new economic crisis and increased job insecurity, both factors rooted in the de-industrialisation processes and globalisation of the 1980s.

In this context, we can also find the position of V.E. Parsi[21], who

---

[18] S. Levitsky and D. Ziblatt, *How Democracies Die*, Crown, New York, 2018.

[19] G. Sartori, *Democrazia e definizioni*, Il Mulino, Bologna, 1957.

[20] I. Kershaw, *Roller coaster*: Europe 1950-2017, Penguin UK, London, 2018.

[21] V.E. Parsi, *Titanic. Il naufragio dell'ordine liberale*, Il Mulino, Bologna, 2018.

argues that the West's difficulties stem from the collapse of the former balance between democracy and the free market in which the two poles corrected each other, finding a balance that benefited society as a whole. It was in the second half of the 1980s that decisions were taken favouring the emergence of an aggressive neoliberalism based on the bulimia of capital and the domination of financial power. This, according to Parsi, brought democracy and its values to its knees, leaving room for the affirmation of populism and the emergence of despotic or authoritarian powers. Slavoj Žižek[22] had earlier put forward the important idea that the link between democracy and the market economy might be broken. According to him, capitalism has readily adapted to authoritarian regimes and cultures which are profoundly different from the Western model, thus showing itself to be more exportable than the democratic political model: the Chinese model of capitalism without democracy is more attractive than it might appear[23]. E. Luce also has the same kind of concern[24]: he argues that "unless the West can rekindle an economy that produces gains for the majority of its people, its political liberties may be doomed". And he also adds that "the West's faith in history teaches us to take democracy for granted (while) reality tells us something troublingly different".

Authors with international clout are also heading in the same direction. Nobel laureate J. Stiglitz[25] continues his analysis of a capitalist system that, according to him, works only in favour of some

[22]See Corriere della Sera, 3 February 2015.

[23]Some observers have explained how China has used the Covid-19 pandemic to launch a propaganda campaign to exalt the authority of its model of government which defeats the virus, as compared with the chaotic and incapable West: see St. Falletti's investigation in Le Figaro of 17 April 2020. But French President Macron responded authoritatively by stressing that one should not be "so naive as to say that China has been much better at handling this. There are clearly things that have happened that we don't know about": see the interview in the Financial Times of 16 April 2020.

[24]E. Luce, *The Retreat of Western Liberalism*, Little, Brown, London, 2017. The book spends a lot of time analysing the situation in the USA and the effects of the Trump administration. It is important to note that the author considers "arrogance towards society's economic losers, and complacency about our system's durability" to be dangerous attitudes and destroyers of our values.

[25]J. Stiglitz, *People, Power, and Profits*, Penguin, London, 2019.

and not for the general good: although this is spreading, it is specifically characteristic of the United States, where the ideology known as neo-liberalist, with its blind faith in the self-regulation of markets, has established itself everywhere, even among judges. According to Stiglitz, nowadays the US economy is based on magnates and oligopolies, with increasingly large concentrations in various sectors: an "inherited plutocracy". But the problem is even more serious than it appears because it has been shown that concentrations of economic power lead to the concentration of political power and this, according to Stiglitz, is already observable in particular (but not only) in the technology sector. The idea that we are confronted by a capitalist system which favours only a few is also supported by T. Piketty[26], a successful author (with millions of copies sold), who focuses, even more than Stiglitz, on the idea that this is the result of a clear ideological choice in favour of neoliberalism and, like Stiglitz, stigmatises the system of inheritance.

Mario Vargas Llosa reacts with annoyance at the spread of the term neo-liberalism. In an interesting interview[27], Vargas Llosa says that the term "neoliberalism" means nothing: it caricaturises liberalism as ruthless capitalism, exploiting deformations that he argues do exist but do not affect the nature of liberal thought, which according to him is not an ideology. The author goes deeper still: in his opinion[28], liberalism puts the responsible individual at the centre of the system and assumes that freedom is the supreme absolute value, while democracy is the system that best manages to reconcile the contradictory values of society.

So liberalism rejects both collectivism and nationalism and above all what the author calls "the tribal spirit" which feeds precisely those ideological choices. This an echo of what we find discussed at length by E. Fawcett[29], who also argues that liberalism is not an ideology, but a basic idea that evolves and is built using new findings: by adopting practices of government and production, liberalism has suc-

[26]T. Piketty, *Capital et idéologie*, Seuil, Paris, 2019.

[27]M. Vargas Llosa, *La corrección política es enemiga de la libertad*, El País semanal, Entrevista, 25.2.2018.

[28]M. Vargas Llosa, *La llamada de la tribu*, Alfaguara, Barcelona, 2018.

[29]E. Fawcett, *Liberalism. The Life of an Idea*, op. cit.

ceeded in holding together the complex societies of the modern age and supporting the people who have no power. According to Fawcett, democracy and welfare are the foundations of liberalism, the pillars that support it in a solid alliance: today, both these pillars are under attack and this undermines the stability of the system. Fawcett concludes that only politics can counteract decline, in the sense that liberals are those who recognise the primacy of politics in human affairs. In a certain sense, we can compare this approach to that of Fukuyama, who disputes the idea that antagonism towards democracy arises out of the economic crisis: Fakuyama attributes this to a search for "identity" that the market cannot satisfy[30]. At the 2020 Munich Security Conference, Francis Fukuyama warned that the rise of identity politics is a threat to democracy: "I am a big believer in democratic governance and I think that all over it's under threat". He went on to say: "We went through this long period where the number of democracies expanded all the way back to the 1970s but we have been in a reversal, or a democratic recession for maybe 15 years, and there's a lot of troubling things that have been going on, including in my own country, the United States, that are not good for the future of democracy." It's all about us (and only us): "I think we are unfortunately moving into an age where politics is going to be defined by identity, which means who I am is really the skin colour, the ethnicity, the religion I was born into. And one country after another is retreating into a kind of closed system," Fukuyama said[31].

All of the analyses referred to so far converge, however, on one thing. That is that these phenomena favour the development and consolidation of so-called (nationalist) populism, which is characterised by an aggressive attack on the elites, by simplistic political language and by the exaltation of the nation state as an identity. This is the idea that people are "waking up" to question the relationship with those who exercise power and claim their own sovereignty, which turns into politics. During the 2019 European election campaign,

---

[30]F. Fukuyama, Identity. *The Demand for Dignity and the Politics of Resentment*, Farrar, Straus and Giroux, New York, 2018. See POLITICO Brussels Playbook, 16 February 2020.

[31]This is exactly the reporting, word for word, by POLITICO Brussels Playbook, 16 February 2020.

some populist-sovereigntist parties explicitly said that they wanted to apply this approach to the European Union and to win the elections in order to take the reins of the EU using this approach. The project did not come to fruition: the result of the May 2019 elections was a European Parliament made up of seven political groups, four of which are openly pro- European and together make up almost 71% of the political spectrum, plus the extreme left, which certainly does not present itself as openly anti-European, while the groups which are overtly Eurosceptic and sovereigntist are two, accounting for a total of 19.5%. of MEPs[32]. This is an important fact, but it must not give rise to an optical distortion which prevents us from seeing the challenges we have to face: the sovereigntist demands remain. The unease about European choices exists, as does the distance from citizens, despite the increase in electoral participation. The weakening of democracy is evident. The fears have certainly not gone away. And even an idea of Europe for the future is not a solid thing. In short, what I want to stress is that from a "political" point of view the question remains completely open.

It is indeed a "political" event which has given much weight to all the observations mentioned so far. At the end of June 2019, during the G20 in Osaka, among the many interesting things that happened there was one that has a greater importance for the purposes of our analysis: Vladimir Putin's statement, in an interview with the *Financial Times* on 28 June reported in newspapers around the world, in which the Russian president said that the liberal values of the West are obsolete. Liberal ideology is now in conflict with the interests of the overwhelming majority of the population who find support and safety in the populism and sovereignty which are gaining ground in Europe and America. Wanting to defend the rights of immigrants instead is an unjustifiable error, according to Putin. Populism and sovereignty, Putin says, are the result of resentment against immigration, multiculturalism and values[33], to the detriment of religion.

[32]Confirmed after Brexit and the departure of the British MEPs.

[33]Unfortunately, the validity of the values of liberal democracy, which are expressed in fundamental rights, is also called into question in theory. J. Lacroix - J.Y. Pranchère, *Les droits de l'homme rendent-ils idiots ?*, Editions Seuil, Paris, 2019, analyse all the elements that underpin the criticism of human rights, such

Russia is certainly not a country known for its liberal thought and politics, so the solidity of Putin's line of argument is questionable. But the real point here is that in this interview Putin presented the authoritarian illiberal model as a model for the future, in front of the whole world, arguing that it is in the ascendant everywhere, starting with the US. Indeed, it must be said that the regression of democratic systems is starting to spread, including within the European Union. And yet the reaction in the West has not been as broad as this claim (the presentation of the authoritarian illiberal model as a model) deserved, either at political level (with the exception of brief statements by Macron and Tusk[34]) or at the cultural level. But when detailed comments have been put forward[35], they have met with silence, because the idea prevails that we are faced with "illiberal" yet democratic systems, not with new-generation despotism. What is meant by the term illiberal democracy is not at all clear, if we exclude election periods where it is also possible to discuss whether they are really free: what I mean is that G. Sartori was probably right when he argued (as mentioned above) that in the end an illiberal democracy would remain an empty shell, since we would be left with the illiberal without the democracy. N. Urbinati goes further. She stresses that expressions such as illiberal democracy, authoritarian democracy, technocratic democracy and so on, are oxymorons, because a democracy which infringes basic political rights and precludes the formation of new majority, is not a democracy at all: this terminology, she says, contributes to a delegitimation of democracy[36].

Another acute thinker of our time, Daniel Innerarity, proposes an

as the dissolution of social ties, neoliberal domination, the end of the political and the selfish claim: the book takes apart these criticisms one by one, showing that they lead to an authoritarian temptation, masked by the concept of "illiberal" democracy. This concept makes no sense, according to the authors, because democracy is not the expression of the majority will but the guarantee of pluralism based on the rule of law.

[34]The President of the French Republic and the then-President of the European Council, respectively.

[35]For example, Nadia Urbinati in *Corriere della Sera*, 8 July 2019.

[36]N. Urbinati, *Introduction*, in N. Urbinati (ed.), *Thinking democracy now. Between Innovation and Regression*, Feltrinelli Editore, Milano, 2019.

extremely interesting interpretation[37]: the problem of modern democracy is that of "mismatching", that is to say it is out of phase with some (or various) evolving processes, for example (but not only) with respect to sovereignty, territoriality, autarchy, etc. The author looks at various aspects, institutions, politics, and citizens. As far as institutions are concerned, one of the most significant changes – he says – is that rulers in the past acted before a mass of people who knew little, whereas today the governed have a high capacity of knowledge: we are witnessing an era in which the institutions which previously were used to giving orders now spend most of their time learning. On the political level, Innerarity tells us, the most worrying phenomenon is the tendency to simplify – in terms of both language and message – complex things, for the sole immediate aim of getting (re)elected. On the citizens' level, the author says, we are witnessing a concept of popular sovereignty which is no longer based on self-limitation but, on the contrary, on the elimination of limits: with the risk of unreflected and disorderly actions.

Does this mean that all the previous analysis should lead us to talk about a "crisis" of democracy? Perhaps. Nevertheless, in my opinion, rather than speaking of a crisis of democracy, we should talk about "new challenges" for democracy. Indeed, as has been said, "Today's dissatisfaction with established democracies is met with proposals for institutional refurbishment, not substitution[38]".

Finally, we must not forget that the European Parliament is an

[37] D. Innerarity, *Una teoría de la democracia compleja.* Gobernar en el siglo XXI, Galaxia Gutenberg, Barcelona, 2020.

[38] N. Urbinati, *Introduction*, op. cit. The same writer puts forward an optimistic view in another essay, N. Urbinati, *Io, il popolo. Come il populismo trasforma la democrazia*, il Mulino, Bologna, 2020, where she rejects the idea that democracy is dying, to argue instead that we are in a delicate period of transformation. The crisis – which is real - is due, she says, to entrenched political parties and policies which have alienated those parties from the citizens. The void has been filled by the populists (whose approach she analyses in depth), but the ground lost could be won back by opening up to participation and citizens, renewing the nature of representation, the essence of democracy. N. Baverez, *L'alerte démocratique*, op. cit., argues that we need to "reinvent" democracy, something which has in fact proved possible historically on several occasions. The author refers to de Tocqueville in order to remind us that freedom is never acquired once and for all, but has to be won every day while taking into account new challenges.

example of non-traditional democracy, since it is a supranational democracy and therefore not rooted in the nation state. We are reminded of this by M.J. Martinez Iglesias[39], who illustrates the path of the European Union's accession to democracy: after being characterised from its origins by the so-called "democratic deficit", it has arrived at the present model of a very advanced representative parliamentary system. The author stresses that the EU "does not automatically generate patriotic support from citizens, [the EU] is justified mainly by its results": a legitimacy based on results can produce only an unstable adhesion. This is why, the author says, the EU is very much focused on governance instruments, such as better law-making, legislative planning, impact assessments and ex-post evaluation of the legislation and stakeholder consultation. And yet, she adds, "democracy reduced to the national level is not possible anymore" because global phenomena erode the ability of the States to take effective decisions. In that context, says Martinez Iglesias, "the political crisis of national democracies is also the consequence of the technological revolution, which is radically transforming knowledge and communication", and put traditional methods of political deliberation under pressure. She ends her analysis by saying: "My conclusion is that the European Union represents an opportunity to improve democracy (or even to save it)".

These last observations by Martinez Iglesias are of the utmost importance, also from a theoretical point of view: I believe, in fact, that in order to face all the challenges for modern democracy analysed so far, we must take as our starting point the fundamental values of the European Union, because it is in them that the solutions are to be found: it is the deep humus of the common European culture which gives birth to the elaboration and maturation of what are the profound values of Europe, those which characterise its specific nature. The founding values of the Union are democracy, law (and rights), freedom, social justice, diversity, and peace (Nobel Prize 2011), all together and not as alternatives[40]. These values break down into a

[39]M. J. Martinez Iglesias, *The Accidental Democracy*: A European Model, in Garben-Govaere-Nemitz (ed.), *Critical Reflections on Constitutional Democracy in the European Union*, Hart Publishing, Oxford, 2019.

[40]See R. Dahrendorf, *Erasmiani. Gli intellettuali alla prova del totalitarismo*,

thousand rivulets and must be properly communicated and defended. For a European:

(1) at the centre is man, his inviolable dignity, his inalienable rights. Women and men have the same rights;

(2) there is a common goal: peace and freedom, democracy and the rule of law, mutual respect and responsibility, welfare and security, tolerance and participation, justice and solidarity;

(3) autonomy and the manifold traditions must be preserved, while open borders and the lively variety of languages, cultures and regions are to be seen as factors for enrichment;

(4) the growing interdependence of the world economy and the increasing competitiveness on international markets must be shaped according to our concepts and values;

(5) we must commit ourselves to ensuring that conflicts in the world are resolved peacefully and people are not victims of wars, terrorism or violence;

(6) freedom and development in the world must be promoted, poverty, hunger and disease must be overcome, and we should play a leading role in this;

(7) in energy policy and climate protection, a contribution must be made to averting climate change;

(8) terrorism, organised crime and illegal immigration should be fought on a joint basis and civil rights and liberties must also be defended by standing up against those who oppose them;

(9) racism and xenophobia should no longer have any chance in Europe. Without the European Union, the process that leads to the erosion of democracy and its decline would have already

---

Laterza, Roma-Bari, 2007. But to understand the specificity of Europe compared with other regions of the world, see the unsurpassed M. Telò, *L'Europa potenza civile*, Laterza, Roma-Bari, 2004.

begun to triumph: it is now clear that it is only thanks to the existence of the EU that national (authoritarian) illiberal pressures have been able to be stemmed, because the European level is the one at which the values of democracy and freedom can be defended: it is clear, therefore, why Europe is the prime objective of those who want to bring down democracy and why the Europe of democracy is our main bulwark[41].

[41]I have developed and explored this approach in G. Vilella, *Being European*, (Foreword by Klaus Welle), Nomos, Baden-Baden, 2017, especially at pp.101-105.

791
790

Chapter 2

The political impulse of the plenary

On 17 October 2019 in his first speech before the European Council, the President of the European Parliament, David Sassoli[1], made the following statement, which is of major importance for our analysis: "*We need a Europe in which the people feel their voices are heard*". This statement very much implies the idea of a European Parliament working with the tools of eDemocracy. Moreover, this is true even more if we place this statement in the context of other important passages of President Sassoli's speech. He said that, in the European elections of May 2019, EU citizens "*issued a call for a new Europe, which is more attentive to their needs, is greener, is more resolute in safeguarding the rule of law, is more protective of social rights, and is more effective and transparent in its decision-making". He went on to state that "the European Parliament is not a dysfunctional brake on the decision-making process; rather it is the basis of legitimacy for the European democratic system*". Lastly, as a consequence, he stressed the initiative of the European Parliament calling for "*a conference on the instruments of democracy in Europe*". Also, in his speech to the

[1]President's Speech at the European Council, Brussels, 17 October 2019. https://www.europarl.europa.eu/the-president/en/newsroom/presidents-speech-at-the-european-council

management of the European Parliament[2], President Sassoli put the question "what do citizens want from us" as the focus of his reasoning. He further dwelt on the Conference on the Future of Europe, which he described as "an important work programme to relaunch the process of development of European democracy", in a general sense and not only as regards the institutions of the Union. So:

- how can we ensure that "people feel their voices are heard"?
- how can we be "more effective and transparent in the decision-making process"?
- what are "the instruments of democracy in Europe"?

All those are big challenges that can be tackled, thanks *also* to technologies, in the context of the concept of eDemocracy. Let us look for the answers by examining the impulses that have been handed down at the political level in this connection.

In its Resolution on "*eDemocracy in the EU: potential and challenges*[3]", the European Parliament gives many inputs for the development of eDemocracy and aspires to play the role of a leading actor in this field. Parliament adopts a "political" definition of eDemocracy, by stating that it is a support of traditional democracy and not an alternative approach. eDemocracy, according to Parliament, provides additional means to increase transparency, participation and openness, through specific tools aiming to empower citizens. Those tools are mentioned in the resolution:

e-government
e-governance
e-deliberation
e-information
e-consultation
e-participation
e-decision making
and e-voting.

[2]Speech given during the 2020 EPA Management Innovation Day: *A Strategic Execution Framework for the European Union*, in Brussels, on 10 January 2020. The title of the President's speech was "An Ambitious Agenda for the European Union". 56 P8_TA(2017)095, 16 March 2017.

[3]P8_TA(2017)095, 16 March 2017

This enumeration has been drawn up after studying the text since that it does not exist in the resolution itself in the form of a list: it will be fundamental when we develop the section on possible prospects. Just two months later the Plenary revisited these instruments on the occasion of the approval of Parliament's resolution of 16 May 2017 on the EU eGovernment Action Plan 2016-2020[4]. Once again we find a list of tools, apart from the term eGovernment, which is regularly mentioned since it is the subject of the resolution. In paragraph 9 alone, we find clustered together eParticipation, eConsultation, eInformation, and eDecision- Making, with many others referred to elsewhere in the resolution: eLearning, eJustice Portal, eIDAS, eCODEX, eSENSE, etc. and more specifically eProcurement, eSubmission and eNotification. In the meantime, it is important to note that Parliament stresses the fact that some conditions are needed in order to make those tools into a successful means: creating people's trust in digital tools[5], organising training and education to eliminate the digital divide and promoting campaigns for the introduction of the new tools. Only in this way, according Parliament, can discriminations be avoided[6]. According to the resolution, we are in an age of increasing disaffection on the part of citizens towards politics, so there is a clear need to improve the democratic link between institutions and citizens, who need to express themselves more frequently and more directly: citizen involvement is now judged to be essential for the functioning of democracy. To cope with this situation, Parliament considers "that digital democracy tools can help promote more active citizenship, improving participation, transparency and accountability in decision-making, strengthening control mechanisms and knowledge".

The European Parliament did not confine its reflections to this resolution on a general concept of eDemocracy. Parliament has explored specific fields in depth in several other resolutions in which it has come up with concrete recommendations and requests. It is im-

[4]European Parliament resolution of 16 May 2017 on the EU eGovernment Action Plan 2016-2020, P8_TA(2017)0205.

[5]This includes (cyber)security on personal data and encrypted identity: we shall be reverting to this issue.

[6]Special attention is given in the resolution to e-voting conditions: reliability of ballots, secrecy, free suffrage, total access. We shall be reverting to this issue.

portant for the present report to point to at least the most relevant of them: I shall do this in chronological order.

The first concerns the role of big data in the economy[7]. In this resolution, the European Parliament points out that big data analytics may potentially accelerate significantly the development of innovative public services based on the use of *open government* data and the reuse of public-sector information. Parliament therefore welcomes the opportunities that digital infrastructure and the integrated use of data bring to increase popular participation and involvement by means of various forms of *e-governance and e-democracy.* Even more, the EP calls for the stimulation of initiatives to increase citizens' awareness of the benefits and value of digital technologies, particularly the use and value of their data.

The second relevant resolution of the European Parliament is concerned with public access to documents[8]. Here Parliament recalls that Article 10(3) TEU recognises *participatory democracy* as one of the main democratic principles of the EU. For the purposes of its implementation, Parliament considers that citizens must have the right to know about and scrutinise the actions of their representatives and the decision-making process (including any documents circulated, individuals involved, votes cast, etc.). Consequently, Parliament urges the EU institutions, bodies, offices and agencies to develop a more proactive approach on transparency by disclosing as many of their documents as possible, in the most simple, user-friendly and accessible way, *including by digital and electronic means.* More specifically, we can read in this resolution that Parliament believes that the EU should make full use of the potential offered by new technologies (social networks, smartphone applications, etc.) in order to ensure complete and easy access to information.

Another important resolution relates to the "Europe for Citizens programme"[9]. In it, the European Parliament stresses the need to

---

[7]European Parliament resolution of 10 March 2016 on Towards a thriving data-driven economy, P8_TA(2016)0089.

[8]European Parliament resolution of 28 April 2016 on public access to documents (Rule 116(7)) for the years 2014-2015, P8_TA(2016)0202.

[9]European Parliament resolution of 2 March 2017 on the implementation of Council Regulation (EU) No 390/2014 of 14 April 2014 establishing the Europe

enrich the programme by proposals on citizens' participation in the democratic process and in EU decision-making in a way that contributes to empowering citizens to make use of their rights, for instance *through the implementation of e-democracy.* It also calls on the Union and its Member States, in order to achieve this, to develop actions and policies to strengthen transferable, critical and creative thinking skills *as well as digital and media literacy.*

Parliament's resolution on the EU Youth Strategy goes in the same vein[10]. In it, Parliament clearly draws attention to the potential of technology for connecting with young people and calls on the EU to strengthen its capacity to participate in society through *e-platforms.* More specifically, the Parliament believes that the EU should express solidarity with young people and continue to empower them to participate in society by developing new tools, especially those *involving new technologies.* Consequently, Parliament recommends that the future European Youth Strategy should be participatory and centred around young people and improving well-being, reflecting the needs, ambitions and diversity of all young people in Europe, while widening their access to creative tools involving new technologies.

I would give one last example: the resolution on the European Citizens' Initiative[11]. In this resolution, it is stated that, in order to make the European citizens' initiative more accessible, the Commission should provide information, assistance and practical support to citizens and groups of organisers, in particular on those aspects of the relevant regulation that are within its competence. To reinforce this information and assistance, the Commission should *make an online collaborative platform* available that provides a dedicated discussion forum and independent support, information and legal advice about the European citizens' initiative. But also, in addition, there is to be a public website providing comprehensive information, a central system for the online *collection of statements of support* and the use

for Citizens programme for the period 2014-2020, P8_TA(2017)0063.

[10]European Parliament resolution of 31 May 2018 on the implementation of the EU Youth Strategy, P8_TA(2018)0240.

[11]European Parliament legislative resolution of 12 March 2019 on the proposal for a regulation of the European Parliament and of the Council on the European citizens' initiative, P8_TA(2019)0153. Note that this is a legislative resolution.

of *digital technologies* and social media in order to raise public awareness about the European citizens' initiative and in the framework of actions to promote Union citizenship and citizens' rights, and so on.

It is very evident indeed that, at the political level, the European Parliament has a clear vision of the potential of new technologies for developing and strengthening democracy through fundamental support for different fields of activities. In the examples summarised above, Parliament refers on several occasions to eDemocracy and links it to the use of new technologies. The list of the sectors on which Parliament considers that new technologies can produce positive effects is of major interest:

- open government
- transparency
- the exercise of citizens' rights
- participation
- creativity
- collaboration[12].

It is possible to observe at this point that the European Parliament has a homogeneous approach to eDemocracy and that it is a coherent and positive vision of its prospects.

It is interesting and important to add that during Parliament's hearings of the candidates for the posts of Commissioners, in 2019 all the items analysed in this chapter were very much at the centre of the debates. They are of major interest for our analysis, i.e. developing eDemocracy, but obviously they are not the only ones[13]. The digitalisation process and new technologies were probably mentioned in all the hearings; however, some of the points raised are particularly relevant for our analysis. M. Vestager said that is fundamental to give people confidence in digital transformation and to build people's trust in technology. She also announced a Digital Services Act

[12]We find all these concepts set out in a concentrated way in the European Parliament resolution on the EU eGovernment Action Plan 20162020, cited above.

[13]Other key items raised in the hearings included digital education, digital taxation, e-health, digital innovation in transport and the digital internal market. For a wider analysis of the all policies orientations of the new Commission, see: EPRS, *The von der Leyen Commission's priorities for 2019-2024*, authored by É. Bassot, January 2020, PE 646.148

on digital platforms, services and products, as well as on regulating how the companies collect, use and share data[14]. V. Jourová engaged in a wide-ranging discussion of strengthening democracy and transparency in Europe and stressed the questions of controlling platforms for disinformation, combating online hate speech, an electronic register for the European Citizens' Initiative and the means for improving transparency and access to documents[15]. J. Hahn emphasised that it is not just a question of digitalisation within the Commission, it is also a matter of interoperability with the systems of Member States and Institutions owing to the very varied landscape of IT systems[16]. D. Šuica concentrated very much on the important Conference on the Future of Europe, stressing that participation in this conference will be not only in person but also online, which means that all materials will be easy to access[17].

This matter warrants a more detailed appraisal[18]. First, Commission President Von der Leyen in her opening statement before the European Parliament on 16 July 2019[19] expressed the wish to involve

[14]In European Parliament, *Commitments made at the hearings of the Commissioners-designate*, Brussels, November 2019, p. 12.

[15]ibid., pp. 28-30.

[16]ibid., p. 41.

[17]ibid., p. 32.

[18]For an analysis of the preparatory steps for the Conference, see the briefing by S. Kotanidis, *Preparing the Conference on the Future of Europe*, EPRS, December 2019, PE 644.202. I should like to take a step backwards at this point by recalling that 2017 was the year in which, after a long period of negative pessimism, a new, positive debate on the relaunch of the European Union was initiated. This was seen both in the media and politically, with articles and speeches containing new proposals, all with a renewed desire to relaunch the EU. The most important and significant of these interventions to give new impetus to the European idea was that of the new French President, Emmanuel Macron: first with a programme-setting speech in Berlin and subsequently on various occasions and in interviews, Macron relaunched the debate, receiving positive reactions from European governments, with Germany and Italy heading the list. The President of the European Commission, Jean- Claude Juncker, also joined this positive movement in his September 2017 speech to the European Parliament on the State of the Union. The European Parliament immediately offered to act as the privileged forum for the orderly development of the debate on the "future of Europe" by organising a programme of meetings and discussions which led to the idea of a Conference.

[19]https://ec.europa.eu/commission/presscorner/detail/en/SPEECH_19_4230

European citizens in the process of the Conference on the Future of Europe as a part of a broader, renewed impulse of European democracy. According to Commissioner

D. Šuica, who is in charge of the process, the inclusion of all citizens' voices will be an essential characteristic of the Conference and, in order to ensure that citizens participate as much as possible, online participation will be fostered. The European Commission has already had quite positive experiences with online consultation[20], and it will help to organise this for the Conference, whilst the European Parliament has launched an in-depth reflection on this matter[21]. This also applies to the participation of local and regional authorities. Moreover, it is worth recalling that the European Parliament, which is at the origin of this important initiative, adopted a resolution on the state of the debate on the future of Europe in February 2019[22]. In that resolution, after a long and detailed analysis of European policies and institutional issues, we find at the end (para. 61) a reference to the need for "providing a platform for reflection and engagement with stakeholders and citizens - with a view to discussing and drawing conclusions from the various contributions to the reflection process and the proposals put forward by (...) civil society and in citizen consultations".

Another resolution more specifically focused on the Conference was adopted by the Plenary in January 2020[23], where Parliament sets out its position on this matter. This resolution is particularly important for our study. First, where (at para. 7) Parliament draws up a (non-exhaustive) list of policy priorities to be discussed at the

[20]S. Kotanidis, *Preparing the Conference on the Future of Europe*, op. cit., mentions some significant examples, at pp.5-6.

[21]I refer to the study for the AFCO Committee, *Potential and Challenges of e-participation in the European Union*, authored by E. Lironi (ECAS) for DG IPOL's Policy Department "C", May 2016, PE 556.949: alongside a theoretical analysis, the study contains concrete examples and operational proposals.

[22]European Parliament resolution of 13 February 2019 on the state of the debate on the future of Europe, P8_TA(2019)0098.

[23]European Parliament resolution of 15 January 2020 on the European Parliament's position on the Conference on the Future of Europe, P9_TA-PROV(2020)0010

Conference, it significantly includes "Digital transformation"[24]. Next, we find many clear statements on the use of new technologies for making the Conference an open and transparent process which takes an inclusive, participatory and well-balanced approach to citizens and stakeholders. Already at the very beginning of the resolution, Parliament advocates the adoption for the Conference of a bottom-up approach to engaging directly with citizens in a meaningful dialogue (para. 2): to this end, citizens' participation and consultations should be organised using the most efficient, innovative and appropriate platforms, including online tools (para. 4). Parliament returns to this also at the end of the resolution where it stresses that all existing and new communication tools for digital and physical participation should be coordinated among the three institutions, starting with Parliament's existing resources (para. 26). The Council of the European Union has reacted rather positively to these suggestions of the European Parliament by accepting (over several paragraphs) among the strategic objectives to be discussed both the idea of involvement of citizens through dialogue and consultation, and the subject of digital transformation[25].

Accordingly, if we summarise the results (which are relevant to this report) of the debates concerning both the election of the new European Commission and the launch of the Conference on the Future of Europe, we find the following aspects which should guide EP work:

- giving people confidence in digital transformation
- building people's trust in technology
- a Digital Service Act on digital platforms, services and products
- regulating how companies collect, use and share data
- controlling platforms for disinformation

[24]Here is the complete list of priorities: European values, fundamental rights and freedoms; Democratic and institutional aspects of the EU; Environmental challenges and the climate crisis; Social justice and equality; Economic and employment issues including taxation; Digital transformation; Security and the role of the EU in the world.

[25]See the note from the Presidency of the Council of the European Union, *Conference on the Future of Europe*, AG32 INST120, Brussels, 24 June 2020, setting out in detail the Council position as agreed at the Permanent Representative Committee.

- combating hate speech online
- an electronic register for the European Citizens' Initiative
- improving transparency and access to documents
- online participation of citizens
- online consultation of citizens
- a platform for reflection and engagement with stakeholders and citizens.

The European Commission, presided by Ursula von der Leyen, received the confidence of the European Parliament and entered into office on 1 December 2019. As it had promised, the new Commission translated all the items analysed above into a Communication, which was presented just over two months later[26]. In this Communication we find the strategy which the Commission intends to follow in the process of the digitisation of Europe : in fact, the DESI 2020 report clearly shows the difference between European countries, some of which are very advanced and leaders, while others "still have a long way to go"[27]. This strategy has three chief axes: technology that works for people; a fair and competitive economy; an open, democratic and sustainable society. Each of these axes breaks down into different key actions. Obviously, in one way or another all the key actions have a link – whether by being ancillary or supportive – with eDemocracy. However, the axis relating to "an open, democratic and sustainable society" is certainly the one most closely linked to eDemocracy. This is because it aims to achieve the following objective: a trustworthy environment in which citizens are empowered in how they act and interact, and of the data they provide both online and offline. A European way to digital transformation which enhances our democratic values, respects our fundamental rights, and contributes to a sustainable, climate-neutral and resource-efficient economy[28]. Among the key actions of this objective, there is one that is particularly important for us: the European Democracy Action Plan. By means of this

[26] *Shaping Europe's Digital Future*, COM(2020)67 final, Brussels 19.02.2020.

[27] European Commission, DG CONNECT, *Digital Economy and Society Index*, Report 2020, https://ec.euro a.eu/di le-market/en/desi: this index summarises, country by country, indicators on digital performance and tracks the evolution of Member States in digital competitiveness.

[28] ibid., p. 2.

action, the European Commission intends to improve the resilience of our democratic systems, support media pluralism and address the threats of external intervention in European elections[29].

Obviously, the emergence of Covid-19 has also influenced Community activity in this area. The President of the European Commission, Ursula von der Leyen, presented her proposals to the Plenary of the European Parliament on 27 May 2020. The European Council, at the meeting held by videoconference on 23 April 2020 in an atmosphere of collaboration aimed at easing tensions, had in fact instructed the European Commission to prepare a plan on the basis of its indications "also with innovative instruments": already on that occasion von der Leyen had made it clear that for the Commission the financial intervention should be structurally embedded in the Community budget and, one month later (as has just been mentioned), presented its proposal before the European Parliament[30]: it has various aspects. The central one is the creation of a recovery instrument "Next Generation EU": this is a €750 billion fund financed on the markets to be repaid over 30 years through the bolstered either by increasing contributions from Member States or, preferably, by creating new own resources, based on new taxes (for instance green taxes and the web tax itself). The instrument will be disbursed partly in the form of grants, in exchange for reforms and investments, and partly in the form of loans. Other parallel actions, such as a new European health programme, will accompany the "Next Generation EU" instrument. As far as the subject of this report is concerned, the Commission proposal states that grants and loans are earmarked, through the implementation of national plans, for the recovery and resilience of the Member States, including "the digital transition[31]". The Commission also stated that, as a consequence of the new situation, its Work Programme would be updated and adapted, while specifying that particular importance is attached to digitisation in the following terms: Europe needs to invest more in better connectivity, and its industrial and technologi-

[29]ibid., p. 12.

[30]See *Recovery Plan for Europe*, online: https://ec.europa.eu/info/live-work-travel-eu/health/coronavirusresponse/recovery-plan-europe_en

[31]Ibid.

cal presence. Technologies such as artificial intelligence, cybersecurity, data and cloud infrastructure, 5G and 6G networks, super- and quantum computers as well as blockchain technologies will have spill-over effects and increase Europe's strategic autonomy. The Commission went on to state as follows on the subject of the real data and digital economy as a motor for innovation and job creation: the Commission will present legislative action on data sharing and governance to be followed by a Data Act. As e-commerce is set to accelerate in the coming years, the Digital Services Act will improve the legal framework for digital services, with clear rules for online platforms. A new Cybersecurity Strategy will boost EU-level cooperation, knowledge and capacity to keep our digital infrastructure safe[32]. The European Parliament has supported the Commission's proposals and plans by a very large majority. Then, in July 2020, the European Council – after a marathon summit – reached an agreement on the European Commission's proposal, with few changes and some improvements, but without changing its structure: this is a decision of great historical importance for Europe[33].

[32]ibid. However, it should be noted that the European Commission has confirmed that, regardless of the Covid-19 emergency and the resulting crisis, the environmental protection agenda remains and will remain a priority. In this regard, L. Floridi, *Il verde e il blu*, Raffaello Cortina Editore, Milano, 2020, analyses in detail how environmental policies and digital technology can merge, focusing on the quality of relationships and processes.

[33]For a detailed appraisal, see also EPRS, Next Generation EU. A European instrument to counter the impact of coronavirus pandemic, authored by A. D'Alfonso, July, PE 652.000

Chapter 3

Possible prospects

In the previous chapter, on the political impulses of the Plenary, we pointed to the tools and the targets that the European Parliament considers at the political level to be fundamental for the correct development of eDemocracy. At this point, we need to understand the conceptual meaning of each of them[1], as well as their practical consequences.

According to the United Nations, "Through innovation and e-government, governments around the world can be more efficient, provide better services, respond to the demands of citizens for transparency and accountability, be more inclusive and thus restore the trust of citizens in their governments"[2]. More specifically, the UN stresses that "Traditionally, e-government has been considered as the use of ICTs information and communications technologies for improving the efficiency of government agencies and providing government services online. Later, the framework of e-government has broadened to include use of ICT by government for conducting a wide range of interactions with citizens and businesses as well as open government data and use of ICTs to enable innovation. E-government can

[1]The bibliography on these questions is immense. Consequently, I decided to make an Internet search for summary definitions. The literature online is also very copious: as a result, I have made choices that I consider to be the most pertinent and useful for our analysis.

[2]https://publicadministration.un.org/egovkb/en-us/About/UNeGovDD-Framework#whatis

thus be defined as the use of ICTs to more effectively and efficiently deliver government services to citizens and businesses"[3]. This definition has been broadly adopted[4] and summarised precisely as follows: "The term consists of the digital interactions between a citizen and their government (C2G), between governments and other government agencies (G2G), between government and citizens (G2C), between government and employees (G2E), and between government and businesses/commerce (G2B)"[5]. This technical definition is extremely useful for our analysis[6].

The United Nations Organisation also adds, however, that "e-government must be supported by an effective *e-governance* institutional framework"[7], thereby introducing the second conceptual tool. The two terms (e-government and e-governance) are often used interchangeably; however, "there is a difference between e-governance and e-government. E-government refers to the use of the ICTs in public administration which, when combined with organisational change and new skills, are intended to improve public services and democratic processes and to strengthen support to the public. However, e-government has no provision for governance of ICTs. The governance of ICTs typically requires a substantial increase in regulation and policy-making capabilities, as well as additional expertise and opinion-shaping processes among various social stakeholders. The perspective of e-governance is the use of the technologies that both help to gov-

---

[3]ibid.

[4]For example, the Organisation of American States says that "the appropriate application of e-Government allows for higher levels of effectiveness and efficiency in governmental tasks, improvement of processes and procedures, increases the quality of public services, also improves the use of information in the decision-making processes and allows for better communication among different governmental offices". See: http://portal.oas.org/Portal/Sector/SAP/DepartamentoparalaGestiónPúblicaEfectiva/NPA/SobreProgramadeeGobierno/tabid/811/Default.aspx?language=en-us

[5]https://en.wikipedia.org/wiki/E-government

[6]In the document produced by EPRS, eGovernment, authored by R. Davies, September 2015, PE 565.890, we read the following statements: "eGovernment refers to efforts by public authorities to use information and communication technologies (ICTs) to improve public services and increase democratic participation".

[7]https://publicadministration.un.org/egovkb/en-us/About/UNeGovDD-Framework#whatis

ern and have to be governed. The central goal of e-governance is to reach the beneficiary and to ensure that their service needs are met. Ideally, the government will automatically recognise the importance of achieving this goal in order to maximise its efficiency"[8].

Two other tools identified by the Plenary as fundamental for the eDemocracy are *e-consultation and e-participation*: the conceptual meanings of the two terms are very close, but there are clear differences, as the following passage makes clear. "E-consultation / Eparticipation are terms used to distinguish two forms of e-democracy. E-consultation involves government-to-citizen and citizen-to-government dialogues. With e-consultation, there exists two-way communications to support information provision and feedback. E-participation involves multi-party communications. With e-participation, there exists multi-directional communications, such as online discussion boards (online forums)"[9]. The following definition goes more into detail as far as e-consultation is concerned: "E-consultation is the use of electronic computing and communication technologies in consultation processes and is complementary to existing practices. E-consultation can be an effective tool in encouraging participation and gathering responses to consultation documents and social policy issues as part of a broader range of methodologies"[10]. As far as e-participation is concerned, it is defined as follows: "the use of information and communication technologies to broaden and deepen political participation by enabling citizens to connect with one another and with their elected representatives. This definition includes all stakeholders in democratic decision-making processes and not only citizen related top-down government initiatives"[11].

---

[8]This very clear definition of the differences between e-government and e-governance can be found at https://en.wikipedia.org/wiki/Egovernance, which mentions P. Rossel and M. Finger, "*Conceptualizing e-Governance*" Management (2007) : 399?407, in ICEGOV07 Proceedings of the 1st international conference on Theory and practice of electronic governance, Macao, Chine, 2007, pp. 399-407.

[9]https://www.igi-global.com/dictionary/democracy/8663

[10]http://e-consultation.org/gide/index.php/E-consultation

[11]https://en.wikipedia.org/wiki/E-participation, which mentions Ann Macintosh (2004). "*Characterizing E-Participation in Policy-Making*", in "Proceedings of the 37th Annual Hawaii International Conference on System Sciences" (HICSS'04), January 05-08, 2004. For a broader list of definitions of eParticipa-

The following two tools, *e-deliberation* and *e-decision making*[12], are what might be termed the corollary of the tools discussed previously in so far as deciding constitutes the end of the process. On one hand, "deliberation is a process within which members of a community engage in discussion on common issues, considering various options for action under the common ground identified between the community members: so, E-deliberation refers to the online performance of all of these related activities"[13]. On the other hand, by e-decision-making is meant "the use of ICT tools and the Internet to involve citizens in policy and public decision-making or in the co-production of services, or to increase the input of citizens in government decision making"[14]. This is supplemented by the other tool mentioned by the Plenary, *e-information*, since this term is defined as "a system which stores information from internal and external sources to facilitate better decision making. The data is collated in a database and the user can access the files to glean better information as a basis for decision"[15].

What is much more complex is the last term enumerated in Parliament's resolutions, that is to say, *e-voting*. The simplest definition of this term is the following: "the application of electronic technology to cast and count votes in an election"[16]. However, it is necessary

---

tion, see also https://www.igi-global.com/dictionary/indicators-measures-government/8868

[12]I find the clarification made by I. Lodewijckx, *What's the difference between deliberative and participatory democracy?*, in https://www.citizenlab.co/blog, 11th September 2019, to be useful and important where she says that: "Deliberative and participatory democracy seem to be pretty similar. And they are because both are democratic systems that give citizens a role in governance"; however, she goes on to specify that "we can state that participatory democracy focuses on empowering citizens to take action, whereas a deliberative system focuses on reaching consensus through discussion, debate and information". The author helpfully adds that "In cases of mass participation, deliberation becomes hard to organise, and equality cannot be guaranteed".

[13]https://www.igi-global.com/dictionary/experimental-deliberation-taiwan/8673

[14]https://www.igi-global.com/dictionary/smart-city-governance/42406

[15]http://www.businessdictionary.com/definition/electronic-information-system.html

[16]https://www.collinsdictionary.com/dictionary/english/e-voting

to add at least the identification of voters[17]. If, on the other hand, we wish to have a complete picture of the concept of e-voting, then the following definition has to be taken into account. "The degree of automation may be limited to marking a paper ballot, or may be a comprehensive system of vote input, vote recording, data encryption and transmission to servers, and consolidation and tabulation of election results. A worthy e-voting system must perform most of these tasks while complying with a set of standards established by regulatory bodies, and must also be capable to deal successfully with strong requirements associated with security, accuracy, integrity, swiftness, privacy, auditability, accessibility, cost-effectiveness, scalability and ecological sustainability"[18].

It seems to me that we now have the sound background knowledge necessary to apply the tools identified by the Plenary for the organisation of the European Parliament. To this end, we need to answer the following questions: what is the governance in the European Parliament? What could be defined as government within the European Parliament? What kinds of consultation and participation are possible? What kinds of decisions could be involved in the process under analysis?

E-governance in the European Parliament

Governance is the way and the system by which an organisation is governed at the highest level. This means especially, as I mentioned above, having regulation and policy-making capabilities, as well as additional expertise and opinion-shaping processes. Accordingly, in the European Parliament the governance system includes:

- the Bureau
- the Conference of Presidents
- the President
- the Secretary General.

We have seen that the prospect for e-governance is the use of the technologies which help to govern, while the central goal of e-

[17] https://www.e-voting.cc/en/it-elections/definitions/
[18] https://en.wikipedia.org/wiki/Electronic_voting

governance is to reach the beneficiaries and to ensure that their service needs are met. Next, e-governance in the European Parliament must guarantee online and electronic interaction[19] with MEPs, other institutions, citizens and the EPA.

E-government in the European Parliament

Since, as we have seen above, e-government refers to the use of ICTs in the public administration, then there is no doubt that this concerns the EPA[20], which includes:

- the Secretary General
- the Management Team
- the Directors General and Directors
- the Middle Management
- the EPA Staff.

As I have mentioned, e-government aims at improving the efficiency of organisation and providing services online. It is also designed to conduct a wide range of interactions with citizens and businesses while providing open government data and using ICTs so as to enable innovation. Accordingly, e-government in the European Parliament must guarantee online and electronic interaction with MEPs, other institutions, citizens and with services within the EPA.

E-governance and e-government in the European Parliament constitute the structural basis for the application of the other tools identified in the political impulse from the Plenary. Having regard to the analysis carried out in the first part of this chapter, the prospective consequences could be described as follows.

---

[19] In this regard, the central role played by the European Parliament in European democracy also emerged during the debate at the conference held at the University of Milan on 9 December 2019, where the emphasis was placed on the importance of the European elections, a topical and centripetal moment in political discourse.

[20] Secretary General K. Welle, in his closing speech for the EPRS Book Talk, *The EPA: strategy and working methods*, Brussels, 8 January 2020, placed the EPA at the heart of the democratic system, in its role as a pillar of the European Parliament, which in turn is a central part of European parliamentary democracy.

E-consultation and e-participation in the European Parliament

Within the European Parliament, this could support the dialogue with staff, as well as inter- services dialogue. Moreover, targeting the involvement of staff in strategic reflections could also be considered as a possible goal. As far as citizens are concerned, providing MEPs with tools for dialogue with citizens and involving them should be an objective, along with providing the EPA with tools for direct exchanges with citizens.

E-deliberation and e-decision making in the European Parliament

As far as the EPA is concerned, e-deliberation and e-decision making could support the involvement of staff in prospective discussions. *Vis-à-vis* citizens, these tools could provide MEPs with tools for involving them in legislative procedures. They can also provide the EPA with tools for mediating contacts between MEPs and citizens.

E-information in the European Parliament

Within the European Parliament, the aim is to create an integrated system for the permanent flow of information to staff and, in parallel, an integrated system for the permanent flow of information as between services. As for citizens, creating an integrated system for the permanent flow of information to citizens, both for institutional activities (MEPs) and EPA activities, is certainly a goal.

E-voting: a very difficult and sensitive aspect

Within the European Parliament, an exercise could be launched for listing some limited fields for electronic vote by the staff (for instance, for the Staff Committee election), as well as listing some limited fields for electronic voting by MEPs outside the Plenary. As for citizens, checking what would be possible, either for consultation or only from a regulatory point of view, could be a useful exercise. Furthermore, all this should take into account the experience made under the pressure of Covid-19 emergency (see farer)[21].

We can now, in the next two chapters, examine what already exists and what is still needed for a broad (or even full) implementation of those goals for the purpose of designing a species of eDemocracy system in the European Parliament. We shall discover that all those aspects are largely covered by the actions of the EPA.

[21]In the Conclusions I will analyse the experience for facing the Covid-19 emergency.

Chapter 4

The state of the art inside the EPA

As I have already intimated, the European Parliament saw the importance of this phenomenon at a relatively early stage. In fact, Directorate-General ITEC, for Innovation and Technological Support, was created in 2007 and endowed with substantial resources, which have been increased over time. The decision to create and set up a Directorate General to deal with new technologies constituted a clear choice in favour of an advanced process of digitisation of the institution. Between 2011 and 2018, a genuine strategic approach was adopted, which aimed, on the one hand, to provide MEPs with the technological tools to strengthen their role and activities and, on the other hand, to foster innovation in the work of the administration. All this was a good fit with a policy context which was based on a clear vision of the future development of the EPA. A large number of actions were actually implemented. After making an in-depth analysis of all the projects carried out by DG ITEC or under the Strategic Execution Framework (SEF)/Parliamentary Project Portfolio (PPP), we can distinguish between three categories of interventions based on technological innovation:

- interventions aimed at making working life easier, both for staff and MEPs
- interventions which help to make work in the European Parlia-

ment more effective and efficient, both for the administration and for MEPs

- interventions that prefigure or even implement aspects of eDemocracy, which are designed to consolidate or strengthen parliamentary democracy

The projects in the third category are primarily of interest to this study.

Let us first consider the projects carried out by DG ITEC which are described in the guide *Innovative Working*[1]. Doubtless, the following projects are intended to make working life easier: use of tablets, Intranet and Mobile Intranet, Directory and Mobile Directory, mobile services and desk services, digital imaging and videoconferencing. As for the following projects, they are designed to make work in the European Parliament more efficient and effective: the knowledge-management programme, collaborative workspaces, remote access and teleworking, cross-media printing and printing anywhere, ICT operational security and encryption, eProcurement and eInvoice.

We now come to the third category of interventions, which are the most relevant for this study and therefore warrant our providing a brief description for each of them, bearing in mind that these are components of a larger programme, eParliament, which (as I shall say later) is structurally essential to the success of the global approach[2]:

- eCommittee: it provides a smart way of working in parliamentary committees by making all information and meeting documents available to MEPs at any time and from anywhere. This working tool is fully supportive of the mobility requirements of MEPs and parliamentary staff. eCommittee is available on any device (e.g. desktops, tablets, smartphones) and any operating system (e.g. Windows, MacOS, iOS, Android).
- eMeeting: this enables MEPs, parliamentary assistants and staff easily to disseminate and share meeting agendas and all meeting documents, for upcoming and past meetings of all committees, in the language of the user's choice. It enables documents to

[1] *Innovative working in the European Parliament. A Guide*, Brussels, November 2016.

[2] In this sense, projects such as ePlenary, eLegislation and so on are also crucial.

be browsed, annotated and shared and last-minute information, such as compromise amendments, to be disseminated. As in the case of eCommittee, eMeeting can be used on tablets, laptops, desktops or even on a smartphone, regardless of the operating system used.

- Drafting Support Tool (DST): this deals with the management of legislative and official documents, which are essential for a well-functioning democracy. Using DST, DLA lawyer- linguists can easily verify, draft and edit amendments, and provide assistance to MEPs with the drafting of amendments.
- AT4AM: it supports the authoring of documents that underpin parliamentary activities. Thanks to this application, the process of creating and managing amendments has never been easier. All the author of an amendment has to do is to enter the text; everything else is taken care of by the application. Authors can easily search and retrieve text to be amended, draft and edit amendments, table amendments to the parliamentary committees and print out amendments in MS Word format for signature, in full compliance with standard document formats.
- Digital Signature (DISP): this was designed to provide a harmonised approach to digital signatures within the European Parliament. Indeed, the real power of DISP lies in its integration with business applications in the IT landscape of the European Parliament - such as WebVisa (used on a daily basis by authorising officers), AT4AM, the Members' ePortal, etc.
- ICT services for constituency offices: with increased external parliamentary activities, Members' Support is extended to local assistants by granting them a nominative IT account: up to two local assistant employees are given access to the European Parliament's ICT systems. DG ITEC extends its services to support the work of Members while they are in their constituencies. The objective is to provide Members and assistants with enhanced remote access to the resources and applications of the European Parliament.
- XML, metadata and indexing: document production is not only about publications in the generally perceived sense. Structur-

ing content, so that it can be successively declined into different formats, or enriching it with consistent metadata, are also of crucial importance for an innovation-led organisation. The processing, and XML structuring of electronic documents is related to the European Parliament's legislative activity. The converted documents are used for the work of parliamentary committees, as well as by the EP website to display the minutes and texts adopted during plenary sessions.
- eVote: this solution makes it possible efficiently to manage all plenary activities from roll-call votes to voting by show of hands and vote-checking procedures. The system registers e-voting session activities and allows the competent parliament services quickly to use the data and information needed in order to report (publish) the results of votes in the plenary.

Let us now carry out the same exercise with the projects actually implemented under the Strategic Execution Framework (SEF) / Parliamentary Project Portfolio (PPP) at the end of the last parliamentary term[3]. However, since a very substantial number of projects (in the order of hundreds) are involved, I shall mention for the first two categories the relevant "programmes" (that is to say, large groups of projects), whilst for the third category (anticipating e-Democracy) I shall briefly describe all those that seem relevant to our analysis. In my view, the projects of the "Enhanced Services" programme and a large proportion of the projects of the "Innovative Working" programme are intended to make working life easier in the European Parliament. Clearly, the projects of the "Managing Efficiently" programme and a large part of the "Linking the levels" and "Completing the legislative cycle" programmes, as well as part of the "Innovative Working" programme, are intended to make work in the EP more efficient and effective. The "Succeeding 2019" programme, which is designed to manage the "before and after" of the European elections, deserves a place of its own.

The third category includes individual projects forming part of the

[3]See the document *Strategic Execution Framework. For the Administration of the European Parliament 2017-2019*, Conclusion SEF 2017-2019, Edition June 2019.

various programmes and a greater number of projects in the "Linking the levels" programme: these projects are still far being from a complete system of eDemocracy as outlined by the impulse from the Plenary, but they are certainly projects which embody elements of eDemocracy or, in any event, anticipate it by accepting its principles and preparing its instruments. Let us see what they are:

- Citizens' Portal & Citizens' App. The purpose is to complement the offer of Europarl by means of a separate application. It provides key information on current EU plans, initiatives and legislative programmes, including the views of civil society organisations and regional actors. Citizens can download documents and share them with their own networks. The application sets out to foster discussion and engage citizens in dialogue, while increasing the traceability of key events and documents[4].
- Consultation of national parliaments on implementation. This supports the goals of ensuring proper linkage within the multilevel governance system of the EU and of agenda-setting, policy formulation and scrutiny and oversight of the executive, by exchanging information with and drawing on the knowledge, experience and priorities of the national parliaments[5].
- Petitions and Citizens' Enquiries review. The aim is to use the information provided by citizens through petitions and citizens' enquiries in order to establish whether their experiences can be taken into account in the process of ex-post evaluation/impact assessment, provide inspiration when amending legislation and enable Members better to use citizens' input in their political work[6].
- EP stakeholder dialogue. This sets out to activate and involve stakeholders in the Member States in the legislative process of the European Parliament: namely, local authorities, NGOs, trade unions, employers' organisations, SMEs and think-tanks situated at a local level with which MEPs have regular contacts and exchanges. Their views might warrant being channelled

[4]ibid., pp. 216-18.

[5]ibid., p. 340.

[6]ibid., p. 348.

into the consultation process carried out by the European Parliament[7].

- URBIS. Digital HUB for consultation. The Unified Repository Base on Implementation Studies is a specialised library, which has become a prime source for information and comparison. Whenever the European Commission announces that it is ready to take the initiative in a specific field, relevant actors (national parliaments and courts of auditors, regional and local authorities, trade unions and employers' organisations, etc.) are invited to deposit their own studies, assessments and strategic visions concerning the same policy field[8].
- Online polling on priorities. It sets out to broaden the rage of tools and platforms used for polling on political priorities. In addition, analysis and presentation of the results should contribute towards better describing the different interests and opinions by country and societal groups. The idea is to allow Members to be informed and obtain valuable insights for strategy[9].
- My House of European History. This is a participative website gathering personal memories from across Europe, allowing users to propose their own content in relation to European History. It is a unique collaborative project incorporating citizens' testimonies: it is conceived as a database of original documents, pictures and videos[10].

There are certainly other projects (such as the various projects relating to the development and use of the EP library) which have to do indirectly with eDemocracy, but those listed above seem to me to be the most significant. I must further point out that the interventions considered in this chapter and to be considered in the next are concerned with projects directly linked to the mechanisms for the institutional functioning of democracy, in which the institution is the primary and creative actor. This is the reason why other instruments are not examined, such as the so-called social media, although they

[7]ibid., p. 356.

[8]ibid., p. 360.

[9]ibid., p. 426.

[10]*Strategic Execution Framework. For the Administration of the European Parliament 2017-2019, op. cit.*, p. 442.

are very important from a sociological point of view in influencing the characteristics of modern democracy. But they do so in parallel, outside the institutions, and for this reason they are not covered by the analysis. However, for completeness' sake, it is good to know that the European Parliament is very present and active in this field: just go to the first page of www.europarl.europa.eu (in any language) to discover that you can interact with Parliament on Facebook, Twitter, Flickr, Linkedin, You Tube, Instagram, Pinterest, Snapchat, and Reddit.

Chapter 5

Operational proposal

At this point we can put together:

- the findings made in the analysis of the political impetus, first and foremost of the EP Plenary, towards eDemocracy (Chapter 2)
- the theoretical and practical consequences of this impulse (Chapter 3)
- the actual achievements of the administration of the European Parliament (Chapter 4)

and make an assessment of what has been done and what could be done in the short term over the coming years (let us say by 2024 at the end of the ninth legislature[1]) in order to satisfy the challenge of eDemocracy in a decisive manner.

A very useful contribution in this sense has been made by the proceedings of the Management Innovation Day, held in Brussels on 10 January 2020[2], when two important publications were put at the disposal of participants to support the debate. The two publications,

[1]However, we must never forget the statement of Secretary General K. Welle in his speech at the EPRS Book Talk, *The EPA: strategy and working methods*, Brussels, 8 January 2020, to the effect that the actions taken "step-by-step are also determined by the political level, which determines how far you can go and at what speed".

[2]2020 EPA Management Innovation Day: *A Strategic Execution Framework for the European Union*, held in Brussels on 10 January 2020.

which are interlinked, were prepared by DG EPRS. The first, *Taking the Pulse*[3], seeks to take stock of existing policy programmes and proposals to date by identifying twelve policy areas deriving from the European Strategic Agenda (June 2019) and the Political Guidelines of the President of the Commission (July 2019), while indicating (with a SEF approach) the degree of progress achieved in meeting the objectives[4]. The second publication, Ideas Papers[5], analyses the twelve policy areas mentioned in the first publication while adding six additional areas and providing a general overview of the topics and exploring possible avenues and options for future actions in the coming years. This was an excellent and useful exercise, which contains at least three topics that are highly relevant for the present study on eDemocracy:

- Linking the levels of Union (EPA Agenda)
- A new push for European democracy (European Commission Agenda)
- Digital sovereignty (European Council Agenda).

The objectives that inspire the actions of "*Linking the levels of the Union*"[6] are concerned with closing the gap with EU citizens and making democracy work better for its citizens. To do so, we need first to map the EU's multilevel governance and then organise the interinstitutional coordination by means of 15 actions divided into 3 sections. All those actions imply the utilisation of new technologies, whereas some of them can be considered explicitly to form part of an eDemocracy structure:

- establishing a regular system of information sharing on EU policy work, including the section on increasing awareness about ongoing EU policy work

---

[3] *Taking the Pulse. A Strategic Execution Framework for the European Union in the making* (K. Welle, ed.; A. Worum, responsible), Brussels, European Parliament, December 2019.

[4] See the Introduction by K. Welle in *Taking the Pulse. A Strategic Execution Framework for the European Union in the making, op. cit.*

[5] EPRS, *Ideas Papers for the Management Innovation Day 2020*, Brussels, European Parliament, December 2019.

[6] Authored by K. Zumer, in EPRS, *Ideas Papers for the Management Innovation Day 2020, op. cit.*, p. 29 et seq.

- the automated digital "sentiment" analysis of publicly available material, as well as consultation on gaps in awareness/misperceptions of EU policy work: both are included in the section on listening in order to understand GOs priorities and concerns
- developing, maintaining and promoting an electronic platform to collect relevant contributions from partners, as well as regular consultations of partners on relevant policy topics: both are included in the section on mutual exchange and input of knowledge and expertise.

The objectives that inspire "*A new push for European democracy*"[7] relate to encouraging and facilitating greater participation in the exercise of democracy, including through citizens' initiatives, the integrity of elections and fighting disinformation. This field includes the goal of involving citizens in the Conference on the Future of Europe. Several actions can be found within this topic, some of them relevant to our research on eDemocracy:

- dialogue initiatives, based on online participation, confronting the problem of possible organised interest domination
- challenging election manipulation carried out using modern technologies
- an action plan against disinformation
- and, as already mentioned, organising citizens' participation in the Conference on the Future of Europe.

The objectives that inspire "*Digital Sovereignty*"[8] have to do with Europe's ability to act independently in the digital world and tackle challenges such as privacy and data protection, cybersecurity and abuses of digital platforms. Europe's ability to do so has four interlinked dimensions: citizens, businesses, Member States and EU institutions. Special importance attaches in this field to the role of

[7]Authored by E. Noonan, in EPRS, *Ideas Papers for the Management Innovation Day 2020, op. cit.*, p. 97 et seq.. See also *Taking the Pulse. A Strategic Execution Framework for the European Union in the making, op. cit.* p. 365 et seq.

[8]Authored by T. Madiega, in EPRS, *Ideas Papers for the Management Innovation Day 2020, op. cit*, p. 203 et seq. See also *Taking the Pulse. A Strategic Execution Framework for the European Union in the making, op. cit.* p. 133 et seq.

Artificial Intelligence[9]. The large majority of the list of 20 possible initiatives proposed are of a legislative (regulatory) nature. If we look for the operational initiatives relevant for our eDemocracy research, we find the following in particular:

- European cloud and data infrastructure
- Joint Cybersecurity Unit
- European Cybersecurity Competence Centres.

The health emergency has accentuated the problem. A careful, in-depth analysis made by the European Parliament of the explosion of digital technologies during the Covid-19 emergency shows the dizzying increase in Internet access, the use of teleworking, recourse to online education, online medical consultations, e-commerce (online shopping), even cultural expressions and online entertainment, and so on. This, however, has accentuated the problems of technological asymmetry (the digital divide) and cyber-security and highlighted Europe's great dependence on external technologies, especially of American and Chinese Big Tech companies[10]. The European Parliament dedicated an academic seminar to the subject of technological sovereignty, focused on identity: from this point of view, it clearly emerged during the seminar that it is necessary to have a precise vision of the balance between centralisation and decentralisation in developing a strategy of technological sovereignty, together with the urgent need to promote widespread digitalliteracy[11]. As the philosopher L. Floridi points out[12], national sovereignty is the State's power of control over its territory, its resources and the legal entities appertaining to it: that is, it is a modern analogue phenomenon and

[9]I shall be returning to this later in this chapter.

[10]EPRS, *How digital technology is easing the burden of confinement*, authored by M. Negreiro, May 2020, PE 651.927. In June 2020, France and Germany took the political initiative to implement a concrete project of technological sovereignty by presenting the Gaia-X platform as an alternative to American and Chinese tech giants, a project that aspires to develop into a European dimension: see IL POLITICO, 6 June 2020. In October 2020, 25 EU Member States had already joined the Gaia-X project.

[11]STOA, *Roundtable on Digital Sovereign Identity*, 11 June 2020, Webex meeting: of course, the technical aspects were also looked into, starting with blockchain.

[12]L. Floridi, *Sovranità Digitale*, in Corriere Innovazione, 31.07.2020 : Floridi is a Professor of Philosophy and Ethics of Information at Oxford University.

concept having its bearings in time, space and physicality.

The contemporary era, however, is above all digital – Floridi says – and this requires a rethinking of the concept of sovereignty by incorporating (precisely) the digital element. But Floridi poses the question, who can exercise digital sovereignty? His answer is that it is not a question of replacing "analogue" national sovereignty, but of flanking it with digital sovereignty, because analogue national sovereignty is no longer sufficient. But, Floridi concludes, the best answer to the control of multinationals over the digital is probably supranational digital sovereignty at European level: in short, it must be organised on two levels.

The European Data Protection Supervisor (EDPS) has also intervened on this issue of digital sovereignty with an initiative concerning the specific action of the European institutions. In a survey launched on its own initiative[13], the EDPS expresses deep concern and perplexity. The EDPS made the following key findings in its investigation. First, the licensing agreement between Microsoft and the EU institutions allowed Microsoft to define and change the parameters of its processing activities carried out on behalf of EU institutions and contractual data protection obligations: the discretion that Microsoft had, amounted to a broad right for Microsoft to act as a controller. Second, EU institutions needed to put in place a comprehensive and compliant controller-processor agreement and documented instructions of the EU institutions to the processors: their lack of control over which sub- processors Microsoft used and lack of meaningful audit rights also presented significant issues. Third, EU institutions faced a number of linked issues concerning data location, international transfers and the risk of unlawful disclosure of data: they were unable to control the location of a large portion of the data processed by Microsoft. Fourth, the EDPS recommended that all EU institutions perform tests using a revised and comprehensive approach, share among them the knowledge and technical solutions they developed to prevent unauthorised data flows to Microsoft and inform each other of any data protection issues they identify with the products or services. Fifth, the EU insti-

[13]EDPS, *Outcome of own-initiative investigation into EU institutions' use of Microsoft products and services*, Brussels, 2 July 2020.

tutions had insufficient clarity as to the nature, scope and purposes of the processing and the risks to data subjects to be able to meet their transparency obligations towards data subjects[14].

Another important contribution in operational terms is the DG ITEC document on strategic orientations[15]. This document is obviously characterised by projects that I have defined in the previous chapter as "interventions that aim to make working life easier or interventions that help make work in the European Parliament more effective and efficient" for both administration staff and MEPs. Nevertheless, the opening part of the document clearly mentions the awareness that "through technological innovation, DG ITEC anticipates the challenges of the future and contributes to a resilient European democracy". After mentioning the objectives of the previous (8th) legislature[16], the document identifies the strategic guidelines for the current (9th) legislature, whereby the aim is to accelerate the digital transformation of the Institution by means of a number of projects.

We find a package of projects designed to increase DG ITEC's ability to be more resilient, open and efficient: service improvement, cybersecurity, metrics collection, contract staff, meeting customers' needs and IT capacity building for democracy support. The latter is directly relevant for the present study: indeed, DG ITEC wishes to help other parliaments become more transparent, accountable and effective through the development of IT governance and the sharing of knowledge. This project is a clear contribution to strengthening parliamentary democracy through a process of digital transformation.

Next, we find a second package of projects calculated to improve the digital workplace (for MEPs, assistants and staff): ICT support,

---

[14]Ibid..

[15]*Information and Communication Technology (ICT) in the European Parliament: Strategic orientations 2019-2021*, authored by W. Petrucci, with the agreement of the Secretary General, D(2019)34304, October 2019. This is a Note to the Members of the Bureau Working Party on ICT Innovation Strategy.

[16]According to the documents, they were: empowering MEPs and streamlining administrative processes; initiating an innovation culture; keeping pace with technology; strengthening ICT security; increasing resilience and business continuity; building on strong partnership.

needs-based printing, ITEC catalogue of services and Parliamentary open data. The latter is directly relevant for the present study: as the document itself says, "the opening up of public data is a fundamental building block of democracy that will help fostering the transparency and accountability of the EU Institutions (...) The project aims to make Parliament more open and accessible to citizens and organisations who want to gain a better understanding of its activities and/or reuse its data".

In addition, there are two other projects, referred to as game changers: that is to say, speeding up the move towards cloud computing and artificial intelligence (AI). The adoption of cloud solutions for the European Parliament will allow new products and services in innovative areas to be procured which are readily available to organisations. This makes it easier to offer more integrated solutions for digital workplaces. On the other hand, artificial intelligence can be introduced for the purpose of supporting specific areas such as machine learning, natural language processing and computer vision. Moreover, other Directorates General in Parliament intend, in the context of the Strategic Execution Framework 2019-2021 ("SEF 2019-21")[17], to use AI to strengthen services or create new ones: DG TRAD has a project on AI in the service of intercultural and language professionals; DG LINC on AI chatbot assistance for conferences; DG COMM on applying AI tools to media intelligence, and DG IPOL on AI and design of future policies. These seem to constitute a very limited utilisation of AI: in actual fact, DG ITEC is aware of the great potential of artificial intelligence and intends to support the exploration and scaling up of AI solutions for the benefit of parliamentary work, engagement with citizens and administrative management, while DG IPOL is working for the implementation of an AI Observatory[18]: the initial aim is to

[17] *Strategic Execution Framework 2019-2021*, http://www.sef.ep.parl.union.eu/sef/cycles/2/home.

[18] As part of this research, I organised a *Study Meeting-Seminar in Artificial Intelligence*, on 3 December 2019, in Brussels. The participants were: Professor D-U. Galetta, University of Milan; Professor E. Francesconi, President of the International Association for AI and Law, and two colleagues from the European Parliament, W. Petrucci (DG ITEC) and M. Maciejewski (CG IPOL), together with S. Angelini, who provided essential assistance. W. Petrucci illustrated, in a

develop tools to address issues of consumer protection and prevention of technological influence on the election process[19]. Indeed, this warrants somewhat more detailed attention[20].

As early as 2017, the European Parliament already decided to seek legislation regulating the sector of robotics[21] and artificial intelligence. In its resolution of 16 February 2017 containing recommendations to the Commission concerning civil rights rules on robotics, Parliament analysed this area in-depth, touching on various aspects: research and innovation, ethical principles, property rights and data flow, security and protection, assistance, the human body, education and work, environment, responsibility and the international dimension. This document is very valuable. Indeed it is essential by virtue of the fact that it draws inspiration from the challenges posed by the development of artificial intelligence. And so it proved to be. On 25 April 2018 and subsequently on 7 December 2018, the European Commission adopted two communications[22] in order to make its approach to this topic explicit and established a group of high-level experts to develop its approach. The Commission's aim is to increase public and private investment in AI[23], to manage the socio-economic changes that come with the adoption of AI and to guarantee an appropriate

---

presentation, the objectives of DG ITEC in introducing AI in Parliament, while M. Maciejewski explained the analysis launched by his Policy Department, possibly oriented towards an AI Observatory.

[19]IPOL, *Role of the European Parliament in promoting the use of independent expertise in the legislative process*, authored by Mariusz Maciejewski, January 2019, PE 626.085.

[20]A very important Workshop has been organised by EPRS/STOA, *The Future of Artificial Intelligence for Europe*, 29th January 2020, EP, Brussels. Hosted by E. Kaili, the Workshop counts on the participation of Commissioner M. Vestager, A. Gooch (OCDE), A. Renda (CEPS) and others.

[21]European Parliament resolution of 16 February 2017 with recommendations to the Commission on Civil Law Rules on Robotics, P8-TA (2017) 0051

[22]COM (2018) 237 final, *Artificial Intelligence for Europe*, and COM (2018) 795 final, *Coordinated Plan on Artificial Intelligence.*

[23]The European Commission is determined to keep up with the pace of the US and China on AI, which are both very advanced in research and funding (China in particular has announced a multi-annual plan worth $140 billion!). For the 2021-2027 budget, the EC has earmarked 2.5 billion euros, while the new President von der Leyen has announced a broader approach in coordination with the Member States

ethical and legal framework. In that regard, the Commission adopts a human-centric vision of AI: artificial intelligence is not an end in itself, but must improve citizen's well-being and be reliable in the dual sense of reliability, being both as technical and trustworthy as people.

On this basis, the expert group produced a document on ethical guidelines for reliable AI[24], which contains all the relevant recommendations as requested by the Commission, as follows. First, it identifies the ethical principles that must be respected: human autonomy, prevention of damage, fairness and explicability, with particular attention being paid to the most vulnerable groups (children, the disabled, those from marginal groups and asymmetrical relationships). Secondly, the document focuses on the seven requirements necessary for AI reliability: human intervention and surveillance, technical robustness and security, confidentiality and data governance, transparency, diversity and equity, environmental social well-being and accountability. Lastly, the document sets out a concrete (but non- exhaustive) checklist designed to make the newly adopted requirements operational[25]. All these constitute fundamental aspects for the correct development of eDemocracy. It may be observed, indeed, that thanks to artificial intelligence, mystification is becoming ever more refined, attaining absolute levels of credibility: today, videos of politicians (or anyone else) making a speech on television or on the web which are a total scam are already difficult to distinguish from reality and will soon be completely indistinguishable from reality[26]. At the end of this first preparatory process, the European Commission adopted a White Paper[27] explaining the lines it intends to follow in order to

[24]Independent High Level Expert Group on Artificial Intelligence, *Ethics Guidelines for Trustworthy AI*, Document made public on 8 April 2019. A first draft of this document was released on 18 December 2018 and was subject to an open consultation which generated feedback from more than 500 contributors. We wish to explicitly and warmly thank all those who contributed their feedback on the first draft, which was considered in the preparation of this revised version.

[25]The expert group has made it clear that the "guidelines" document does not replace the necessary political or legal action.

[26]See EPRS-STOA, *Regulating disinformation with artificial intelligence*, March 2019, PE 624.279.

[27]European Commission, *White Paper on Artificial Intelligence – A European approach to excellence and trust*, Brussels, 19.2.2020, COM(2020) 65 final. See

determine a common approach in the Union to the question of AI: it is clear that this document is also the reference for the European Parliament and its administration. Following a proposal by the Conference of Presidents, MEPs voted to set up a new special committee on artificial intelligence. It will analyse the future impact of AI on the EU economy and investigate the challenge of deploying AI and its contribution to business value. The new committee is a recognition of both the importance of AI and our modern world's direction of travel.

A third fundamental contribution from the point of view of operational proposals for the immediate future with the aim of building an eDemocracy system in the EPA, comes from the Strategic Execution Framework 2019-2021[28]. This document sets out 157 projects divided into nine programmes: Enhanced Services, Managing Efficiently, Digital Transformation, Completing the Legislative Cycle (Reloaded), Linking the Levels, Succeeding Mass Communication, Closing the Expectations Gap through Instant Legislation, Preparing for 2030, and Game Changing Metrics. All the projects are designed either to make working life in the institution easier or to help Parliament act more effectively and efficiently. However, some of the projects can be clearly linked to the idea of prefiguring or implementing aspects of eDemocracy. On the basis of the methodological approach adopted so far, I consider that those projects are the following:

- Citizens' APP go local[29]: it aims to improve European citizens' information about local initiatives taken by the European Union from which they benefit directly. The goal of this project is to enrich the application content with initiatives and specific local achievements supported by the European Union
- Data Driven Communication[30]: it aims at ensuring a more systematic audience- and data- driven approach to communication through processes which ensure analysis of different data

the excellent summary of this document made by DG IPOL, *The White Paper on Artificial Intelligence*, authored by M. Ciucci and F. Gouardères, PE 648.773 – April 2020.

[28] *Strategic Execution Framework 2019-2021*, http://www.sef.ep.parl.union.eu/sef/cycles/2/home

[29] ibid. web page 2

[30] ibid. web page 2

sources, improved dissemination and operational uptake of insights and increased data mindset among staff.

- Parliament Open Data[31]: it will consist in publishing on the Internet, on a dedicated portal, the data sets already available in the parliamentary domain, using an open licence. These and other data sets to be defined will have to be made available in a machine-readable, non-proprietary format.
- Hub with National Parliaments on Democracy Support Activities[32]: the aim of this project is to become a centre of excellence in parliamentary democracy support activities, by developing this expertise at the European level. The platform of best practices could include the following indicators: inter-party dialogue and consensus building; parliamentary mediation; election observation missions; human rights actions and gender rights; young political leaders' support and engagement with civil society; and parliamentary administrative capacity building.
- Partnership with Local Governmental Organisations[33]: this aims at achieving a systemic partnership, including responsive and interactive two-way communication with local government actors. The main goal of these partnerships is to support the European Parliament's analysts with expertise from relevant organisations and with input from people on the ground. Partnerships will be developed with Eurocities and the European Local Authority Network (ELAN), and through closer links with the administrations of the largest EU cities.
- Partnership with Regional Governmental Organisation[34]: systemic partnership, including responsive and interactive two-way communication with regional governmental actors. The introduction of the principle of subsidiarity by the Maastricht Treaty increased the role of regional actors in EU decision-making. Partnerships will be developed with the Council of European Municipalities and Regions (CEMR) and the Conference of Eu-

[31] ibid. web page 8
[32] ibid. web page 6
[33] ibid. web page 8
[34] ibid. web page 9

ropean Regional Legislative Assemblies (CALRE).

- Partnership with National Parliaments on Implementation[35]: systemic partnership, including responsive and interactive two-way communication with national parliaments of EU Member States. National parliaments have an important potential role to play in the implementation of EU legislation at national level.
- Identifying Expectations Gaps[36]: identifying gaps between public expectations and EU delivery, including on the basis of new subjects. Public expectations for EU action are sometimes high in domains where the EU has not yet developed policy responses and/or not yet delivered them to an adequate degree.
- Multiplier Networks Civil Society[37]: the project aims to establish a long-term outreach strategy and stimulate collaboration with multiplier networks on communication projects. It seeks to create opportunities for civil society and other multiplier networks in order to share experiences and practices surrounding the communication of EU-related topics to citizens.
- My House of European History (see also Chapter 4)[38]: the aim of this project is the management and improvement of the platform "My House of European History" as well as the ideation and creation of audio testimonies on the basis of stories sent by citizens to the platform.
- Youth Engagement[39]: the underlying goal remains to encourage young people to participate in democratic life, to give them the opportunity to understand their rights as European citizens and facilitate a genuine dialogue between them and the European Parliament.

I consider that all the above projects, scheduled for implementation during the ninth legislature, are directly linked to the concept of eDemocracy analysed in this report. However, SEF 2019-21 includes a number of other projects that we can regard as being supportive of the tools of eDemocracy: I refer to projects such as EP Archives for the

[35] ibid. web page 9
[36] ibid. web page 6
[37] ibid. web page 8
[38] ibid. web page 8
[39] Ibid. web page 11

Digital Age and the iVote-intelligent voting list[40]. To these projects we need certainly to add Cyber-Security and Cyber Defence[41]: the aim of this project is to improve the capacity for vigilance and reaction against cyber-attacks and assure business continuity. It will also aim at increasing users' maturity in cyber security in their day-to-day activities. A special focus is on cybersecurity culture (through awareness and training for Members and EP users) and systematic and harmonised application of security testing and incident prevention through an efficient IT administration model. This is an essential concern for the purpose of trust in eDemocracy.

[40]To this category of IT projects which go in the direction of achieving a proper "e-Democracy" could perhaps also be added HERMES, the new Electronic Records Management System which will be the gateway for electronic communications in the future with citizens. From this project, sponsored by the GIDOC group, other branches will emerge, such as electronic documents with legal value (electronic contracts), paperless strategy, easier citizen participation in European projects, etc. It falls more in the category of support to eDemocracy tools, but is fundamental.

[41]ibid. web page 2.

Chapter 6

Critical remarks

At this point, we have all the analytical and operational data in order to draw up some critical remarks. This study has shown that the European Parliament is extremely sensitive to the development of eDemocracy, both at the political and administrative levels. Indeed, at administrative level, it has become very clear that the European Parliament's Administration has largely adopted solutions which prefigure or in any event favour a definable approach to eDemocracy: I shall close this report with the list of the things which have been done and of those which are under way. At political level; the concept of eDemocracy adopted by the European Parliament is that of an instrument to support and enrich parliamentary democracy, founded on two major pillars: connecting people and dialogue, based on the "empathy" between citizens and institution. As we have seen earlier (Chapter 2) EP defines eDemocracy, by stating that it is a support of traditional democracy and not an alternative approach: eDemocracy, according to Parliament, provides additional means to increase transparency, participation and openness, through specific tools aiming to empower citizens. Even more: Parliament considers "that digital democracy tools can help promote more active citizenship, improving participation, transparency and accountability in decision-making, strengthening control mechanisms and knowledge" (again, Chapter 2).

The role of the administration in developing that definition and preparing and managing its abovementioned two pillars is essential.

They receive a great boost from the political impetus of the Plenary, from the will of the President of Parliament to build an EU in which people feel their voices are heard (Sassoli) and from the approach of the Secretary General in support the idea of an EU which is closest to citizens (Welle). In short, what emerges from this study is an optimistic view of the integration of eDemocracy into parliamentary democracy. Of course, some might say that this is an "excessively" optimistic vision, that reality is far from what is needed in the sector, that we have to deal with the traditional hostility of public administrations to innovation and, even more, that at present there are more problems than solutions or good practices. It is always important and useful to take such criticism seriously if we want to improve. However, my optimism is based on the facts that I have described and which I will summarise in the conclusions section: it is also based on the fact that there is objective awareness of the issue, the will to try to evolve in this direction and an actual commitment to concrete projects. Substantially, this is optimism about great potential.

Nevertheless, the fundamentally positive approach adopted in this study should not cause us to forget that the risks to democracy arising from new technologies are neither few nor secondary. Already in the first chapter we saw that modern democracy has to contend with

essential challenges[1] and come up with responses which aim at "institutional refurbishment, not substitution" of the system: these challenges consist of internal mechanisms that erode the functioning of democracy, weaknesses in the link and the balance between democracy and the free market, an aggressive attack on elites and the representative system, and many others. In particular we should add: the huge affirmation of the concept of illiberal democracy within an

[1] I closed the first chapter by stating that "in my opinion, instead of a crisis of democracy, we should talk about new challenges for democracy". The essay by W. Merkel, Crisis, Challenges, or Transformation of Democracy, in N. Urbinati (ed.), in *Thinking democracy now. Between Innovation and Regression, op. cit.*, offers us new insights that add to the dilemma as whether we are dealing with a crisis of democracy or new challenges. In the meantime, the author says, if we stick with the idea of a "crisis", we still need to understand whether it is a latent crisis or an acute crisis. But, W. Merkel adds, in truth it could also be a "transformation" or "erosion".

authoritarian approach, the people's difficult search of identity, the mismatching of institutions' action with reality and the situations of (health or terrorist) emergency.

To these challenges must now be added the difficulties arising from the successful achievement of new technologies in our life. In a good summary covering the system as a whole, L. Violante[2] shows how this is no longer simply a matter of innovation, but a real paradigm shift. Indeed, digital society is characterised, according the author:

- by disintermediation,
- by overcoming representation, and in any case by directly downsizing it,
- by direct political decision-making,
- by denial of political elites and knowledge,
- by the propositional referendum in competition with legislation based on parliamentary initiative,
- by leadership based on followers before voters.

All these facts are dangerous for democracy, but, in the author's view, the most dangerous is the claim of disintermediation[3], which in truth is a deception: in fact there are new mediators on the Internet, but they are not visible, they are not scalable and there are no rules or counter powers.

And it is precisely the invisible mediators who exercise F. Foer[4], who analyses how large digital platforms use our data and how they have been able to transform this information into essentially economic value. Foer shows how, starting from this, we discover that those companies are able to influence, or rather change, the way we think, what objects we buy and what politicians we trust, that is to say, our

[2]L. Violante, *Rifondare la democrazia nella società digitale*, in Storia e Memoria, n. 1/2020, p. 123 s.

[3]S. Cassese, *Il popolo e i suoi rappresentanti*, Edizioni di Storia e Letteratura, Roma, 2019, points out that representation as we know it, is not a binary electorate-representative relationship, but a ternary one where an intermediary, mostly a political party, makes the political choices and chooses the candidates: the electorate intervenes at the end to endorse and select the choices made by the intermediary. Democracy began to suffer when political parties lost their ties with society and, as a result, the ternary system no longer functions properly.

[4]F. Foer, *World Without Mind. The Existential Threat of Big Tech*, Penguin Press, New York, 2017.

condition as citizens, consumers and people. G. Lovink[5] thinks on the same lines: according to him, "platforms like Google and Facebook are designed to channel users into forced paths that generate discomfort". These are centralised systems, that is to say, the exact opposite of the idea of a network that is decentralised and distributed, and this centralisation implies total control of the user, who feels trapped, because although he is uncomfortable, he cannot get out of it.

The position of S. Zuboff[6] is on the same lines, but with a different vision: according to her, new technology companies have identified human experience as the new raw material to be monetised, essentially by using the ability to extract elements so as to identify people's future behaviours. Zuboff defines this approach as "surveillance capitalism", which exploits data without authorisation and therefore unlawfully, a species of theft aimed at trading behaviours on the market: something which affects a very large part of economic activities. According to Zuboff, this produces an "epistemic inequality" where some (the technology companies) can know a lot, while the others (the citizens) can know almost nothing about each other's behaviour.

It is no coincidence, therefore, that 2019, but in part also the previous year, was characterised by a growing demand for forms of regulation of large digital platforms. This is the analysis carried out by M. Del Mastro and A. Nicita[7], who recall that many reports have been produced on the risks of monopoly (or oligopoly) in intermediation, on the reduction of pluralism and on strategies of disinformation and misinformation on the Internet (online): authorities, parliamentary committees, research bodies and other agencies in every corner of the world have tried their hand. The common question is whether public regulation is necessary to counter those risks, but also, if our answer to that question is in the affirmative, we will need to understand what the real impact of such regulation will be, since there is

[5]G. Lovink, *Sad by Design. On Platform Nihilism*, Pluto Press, London, 2019.

[6]S. Zuboff, *Il capitalismo della sorveglianza*, Luiss University Press, Roma, 2019. See also, with the same approach, O. Tesquet, *À la trace. Enquête sur les nouveaux territoires de la surveillance*, Editions Premier Parallèle, Paris, 2020.

[7]M. Delmastro – A. Nicita, *Big Data – Come stanno cambiando il nostro mondo*, Il Mulino, Bologna, 2019.

a very real risk of inefficient or distorting results[8]. Before arriving at a valid regulation, the authors say, perhaps it would be useful to activate coordinating authorities to carry out audits and inspections in order to provide all the evidence useful for correct and effective regulation leading to a "new Web".

All these factors must be borne well in mind in the process of developing and implementing eDemocracy tools in the European Parliament, because they entail paying serious attention to ICT security and data protection[9]. Obviously, I do not need to go into these aspects in more detail, but it is necessary to remember that eDemocracy has no future without a sound policy in these two areas.

I could just cite the fundamental adoption in 2016 of the General Data Protection Regulation and the related Data Protection Law Enforcement Directive[10], where the European Parliament played a crucial role together with the European Data Protection Supervisor[11]. And I should add (amongst others) the resolution on the

[8]The most important recent example (as I write) is Mark Zuckerberg's visit to the European Commission in February 2020. The CEO of Facebook went to discuss taxation but especially rules on the Internet, submitting his ideas on this subject: see POLITICAL Brussels Playbook of 17 February 2020, Le Soir of 18 February 2020 and the interview with Monika Bickert (Facebook Vice President for Global Policy Management) in Corriere della Sera of 20 February 2020.

[9]I had the opportunity to discuss in depth the relationship between eDemocracy and Cybersecurity and the relationship between eDemocracy and Data Protection on 15 January 2020 in two separate meetings with P. Paridans (CISO of the EP) and S. Sabbioni (DPO of the EP). These two colleagues made me understand the extreme importance of ICT security and data protection for eDemocracy.

[10]Regulation (EU) 2016/679 of the European Parliament and of the Council of 27 April 2016 on the protection of natural persons with regard to the processing of personal data and on the free movement of such data, and repealing Directive 95/46/EC, OJ L 119, 4.5.2016, p. 1, and Directive (EU) 2016/680 of the European Parliament and of the Council of 27 April 2016 on the protection of natural persons with regard to the processing of personal data by competent authorities for the purposes of the prevention, investigation, detection or prosecution of criminal offences or the execution of criminal penalties, and on the free movement of such data, and repealing Council Framework Decision 2008/977/ JHA, OJ L 119, 4.5.2016, p. 89, respectively.

[11]I would pay tribute here to the European Data Protection Supervisor, Giovanni Buttarelli, who died in August 2019 while in office. His contribution with regard to these issues was substantial, having played a central role in the develop-

Cambridge Analytica case[12], in which the Parliament "notes that the misuse of personal data affects the fundamental rights of billions of people around the globe" (para. 30). The resolution sets out a long list of cases of infringements of personal data, but Parliament focuses very much on the manipulation of elections, a fundamental question of democracy. And we must not forget another aspect, which is the ethics of the management of personal data. In 2018, the EDPS produced a report describing the risks to democracy arising out of the misuse of personal data[13].

With the Covid-19 health emergency there has been the problem of using technology to stop or slow down the contagion: I say "problem" because this use of technology involves the transfer of peoples' personal data (and in any case the exercise of control over it). The country where full use of this approach has been made is South Korea (but also Taiwan), which has become the reference model for many other States, included in the European Union. How does it work? With the help of telecom operators, it is possible for the authorities to obtain information about peoples' movements, to check whether containment measures are being complied with and to create individualised communication channels[14]. It is actually possible to go very far with individual controls by, for example, ensuring that those in quarantine do not move, reconstructing the previous days of the infected and their contacts, identifying peoples' position in relation to

ment of the new GDPR, the European Data Protection Regulation, and he was regarded as one of the world's greatest experts in new technology, privacy and data protection law. In his homage to him - in Corriere della Sera of 23 August 2019 -, Tim Cook, Apple's CEO, said: "Giovanni had an unparalleled ability to relate to all points of view. He never compromised on his own values or the public interest, but he was always able to focus on elements of possible understanding rather than differences". I, who had the honour of knowing him well and working with him in my role as Director General of DG ITEC, subscribe to this precise and intelligent judgement.

[12]European Parliament resolution of 25 October 2018 on the use of Facebook users' data by Cambridge Analytica and the impact on data protection, P8_TA(2018)0433.

[13]*EDPS Ethics Advisory Group, Towards a digital ethics*, Report 2018, European Union, Brussels, 2018.

[14]For these explanations, see the in-depth, documented investigation by M. Gabanelli and F. Savelli in Corriere della Sera of 23 March 2020.

the infected and so forth. These are certainly effective measures, but in these circumstances it becomes impossible to speak of the right to privacy, because it simply disappears[15]. At the request of the European Commission (made through the Internal Market Commissioner, Thierry Breton), the main European telecom operators have indicated their willingness to work together to provide geolocation data collected through mobile phones: Mr. Breton pointed out that these data are collective and anonymous. A few days later, the European Commission formally adopted guidelines on this matter, contained in a Communication[16]. It intends to foster a coherent approach across the EU and to provide guidance to Member States and app developers. This document sets out features and requirements which apps should meet in order to ensure compliance with EU privacy and personal data protection legislation, in particular the General Data Protection Regulation (GDPR) and the ePrivacy Directive, even though the guidance is not legally binding. The Communication takes into account the various aspects, starting from the potential of apps to contribute to the fight against Covid-19: national health authorities as data controllers; ensuring that the individual remains in control; legal basis for processing; data minimisation; limiting data disclosure/access; providing for precise purposes of processing; setting strict limits to data storage; ensuring the security of the data; ensuring the accuracy of the data, and involving Data Protection Authorities. Within this framework, which we can consider complete, the essential point remains that the European Commission states clearly and resolutely that everything must be done on a voluntary basis: in essence apps must be downloaded, installed and used on a voluntary basis by individuals.

[15]A Bva Doxa survey, based on a sample of five thousand individuals, showed that 93% of Italians (or of those polled) are ready to sacrifice some fundamental rights if this helps to prevent the spread of the virus. Much more than this, see Corriere della Sera of 6 April 2020, p. 4: "Chinese citizens (in Wuhan) can only move if the app that certifies their health status shows the green code. It is a QR code in their personal smartphone which has to be placed on the turnstile of the Metro: if the code is green the owner is not a carrier of the Coronavirus. Yellow indicates that the owner must be in home isolation and red that the owner is a Covid-19 patient".

[16]European Commission, *Guidance on Apps supporting the fight against COVID 19 pandemic in relation to data protection*, Brussels, 16.4.2020, C(2020) 2523 final.

If, however, we should want to go further and carry out individual checks which are not anonymous and not previously authorised, as is indeed the intention in some countries, we would need specific legislative action. In order to get around this problem, we are trying to find contractual solutions while choosing the application that satisfies the constraints of privacy protection. As I mentioned in Chapter I, the European Parliament dealt with health tracking in its important resolution on coordinated action against Covid-19[17]. Having taken note of the Commission's plans, its specific recommendation and national programmes, Parliament calls on all actors to act in a transparent manner, more specifically:

- *Calls on the Commission and the Member States to publish the details of these schemes and allow for public scrutiny and full oversight by data protection authorities (DPA); notes that mobile location data can only be processed in compliance with the ePrivacy Directive and the GDPR; stresses that national and EU authorities must fully comply with data protection and privacy legislation, and national DPA oversight and guidance*[18].

The experience of tracking, however, has not exactly been a success in the various European countries or in any case has not lived up to the expectations for which it was designed: tracking has certainly been a help, but it has not been a pillar of anti-Covid action. European Parliament returns to the issue of privacy, also in the resolution on the eGovernment Action Plan[19] by emphasising "that citizens' trust in the protection of personal data is fundamental" (para. 35). In this resolution, on the other hand, Parliament also stresses "that measures to protect public authorities from cyber-attacks and to enable them to withstand such attacks are extremely important and need to be developed" (para. 40). This is just an early example of Parliament's concerns about cybersecurity. One year later, with the resolution on cyber defence[20], Parliament constructed a coherent sys-

[17]European Parliament resolution of 17 April 2020 on EU coordinated action to combat the COVID-19 pandemic and its consequences, cited above.

[18]ibid. para. 53.

[19]European Parliament resolution of 16 May 2017 on the EU eGovernment Action Plan 2016-2020, P8_TA(2017)0205.

[20]European Parliament resolution of 13 June 2018 on cyber defence,

tem by focusing in depth on a series of issues: capability development for cyber defence and deterrence; cyber defence of CSDP missions and operations; cyber defence education and training; EU-NATO cooperation on cyber defence; international norms applicable to cyber space; civil-military cooperation, and public-private partnership. This clear vision of the matter has been the basis for subsequent legislative activities, culminating in the adoption of the EU Cybersecurity Act[21].

One final reflection seems to be worth making before the conclusions of this study. A European Commission internal analysis[22] focuses on political behaviour and raises many issues having a bearing on this report, precisely because they are important to take into account in the implementation stage. The first is misperception and disinformation: we can read in the European Commission's document that today's information environment makes us vulnerable to disinformation, and misinformed people do not think of themselves as ignorant because they are in possession of facts which they believe to be true[23]. The second issue has to do with emotions: the document tells us that better information about citizens' emotions and greater emotional literacy could improve policy making, because angry people are less likely to seek information and more likely to have a closed mind[24]. The third is about trust and openness: trustworthiness depends - the Commission document says - on expertise, honesty, shared interests and values[25]. The European Commission's internal analysis concludes that collective intelligence, better-oriented narrative and framing policy problems are essential tools in order to face the three issues identified. I think, indeed, that this approach will help with the development and the prospects for implementation of eDemocracy.

P8_TA(2018)0258

[21]Regulation (EU) 2019/881 of the European Parliament and of the Council of 17 April 2019 on ENISA (the European Union Agency for Cybersecurity) and on information and communications technology cybersecurity certification and repealing Regulation (EU) No 526/2013, OJ L 151, 7.6.2019, p. 15.

[22]EC Joint Research Centre, *Understanding our political nature*, EUR 29783EN, Luxembourg, 2019.

[23]ibid., p. 11 et seq.

[24]ibid., p. 29 et seq.

[25]ibid., p. 53 et seq.

Chapter 7

Conclusions

We now come to the conclusion of this study, which adopted the (political) concept of democracy put forward by the Plenary of the European Parliament: digital democracy tools can help promote more active citizenship, improving participation, transparency and accountability in decision-making, and strengthen control mechanisms and knowledge (see Chapter 2). This concept has the theoretical (academic) consequence that eDemocracy must be seen as a development of representative democracy in the sense that it extends its borders and therefore strengthens it (see the section on "Scope"). This has given rise to analysis and research focused on aspects and instruments closely related to the aforementioned political concept and theoretical approach. As a result, the actions designed to make working life easier and to help make the work of the European Parliament more effective and efficient, both for the administration and for MEPs (see Chapter 4), have only been mentioned and are not the subject of deeper consideration because they do not constitute the core business of our analysis.

Now: as I mentioned at the beginning of this study (see again the section on "Scope"), the emergence of the Covid-19 coronavirus has made it necessary to search for solutions for the proper functioning of the institution and this in turn meant that we had to reflect on the use of technology in such situations. To a large extent, what we have been looking at is the possibility of effective remote working of MEPs and staff. In this sense, in the midst of the emergency created by the spread of Covid-19, DG ITEC sent an internal note to all staff, entitled "Teleworking facilities", which listed the available possibilities: connecting from your personal laptop; token access for security; email access through webmail; extranet access; jabber access; VDI for remote access; email access on phone or tablet; hybrids. By recalling what the "normal" tools available are, the note implicitly underscores their usefulness in times of emergency[1]. The services then got to work to strengthen these capabilities. The experience of teleworking or smart working during the health emergency has reinforced the positive approach to this method, so that outside the European Parliament many companies and administrations have launched projects for its regulated and "normal" use. A recent study[2], tending to concentrate more on the practical and operational consequences, has shown the specificity of this approach by stressing that smart working is different and much more than teleworking: the first principle is that in smart working the work takes place at the most effective places and times in relation to the needs. Manifestly, this implies a great willingness to be flexible, including the possibility of choosing the best times and places to work. This flexibility, the study tells us, must, however, be managed in terms of behaviour and methods, in order to completely eliminate mediocre performance: workloads, monitoring, reporting, communication, not to mention the necessary adaptation of digital infrastructures. Finally, the study reminds us, the qualities of the teams involved is crucial, because of the related risks that need to be overcome, such as difficulties in time management, loss of team spirit and isolation[3].

---

[1]DG ITEC has returned to the subject once again with a new communication to staff (*Teleworking tools: the essentials*, 31 March 2020), which is even more concrete, holding out a hand, so to speak, to colleagues who were by then working remotely.

[2]R. D'Apolito and A. Fratini, *Smart Working facile* (E non solo), FineAdvisors, published by Amazon Poland, 2020.

[3]Ibid. To return to the European Parliament's experience of teleworking, it is important to remember that to further enhance the well-being of staff while teleworking, as announced at the meeting of the Bureau of 15 June 2020, the responsible Parliament services are assessing staff needs for additional teleworking equipment. This concerns in particular external screens, keyboards, mice and

An initiative taken by the European Parliament's Library was of equal importance. When remote working was fully up to speed, so to speak, it announced that "the European Parliament's Library has prepared a wide-ranging selection of e-books and e-journals for colleagues to consult and use while they telework from home. You can access these materials through your hybrid computer or by Virtual Desktop Infrastructure (VDI) (?) In practice, what this means is that: the digital services of the EP Library – including the catalogue, e-books, databases and journals – continue to be available to Members and staff at all times, on the same basis as before, to the maximum extent possible; the Library Help- desk will continue to be available by email at library@europarl.europa.eu – and will answer reference enquiries for library materials and practical questions about how to access digital library services."[4] In addition to these important initiatives of the Library, it should be borne in mind that the EPRS is a major organiser of events: accordingly, when teleworking became the norm, the EPRS offered several online book talks and this worked well overall. DG COMM took the same approach, holding webinars with MEPs and journalists so as to guarantee continuous media coverage for the European Parliament. On top of this, DG COMM successfully organised a digital European Day (9 May) and EYE Online (25-29 May). Moreover, DG TRAD has continued, not only to serve the institution by ensuring the functioning of its core business, but also to produce citizens' language products for use in information campaigns on what Europe is doing for its citizens during the crisis. Switching almost 100% of DG TRAD's staff to teleworking and completely changing working methods required the coordination and implementation of exceptional measures in the areas of HR and IT[5]. And I could go on

ergonomic chairs. Staff who need it most could receive these items from the existing stocks. As of 7 September 2020, 8063 hybrid devices were deployed, 1249 screens, 994 keyboards and 993 mice were distributed to staff on request: *see Technical Notes for the meeting of the Bureau on Monday, 14 September 2020, PE 653.583/BUR*

[4]EPRS, *Access to e-sources while you are teleworking*, 8 April 2020. This additional service is also described in Newshound, *All these information sources at your fingertips*, Edition 632, 15 April 2020.

[5]In the TRAD Newsletter, TRADIVARIOUS of 12 July 2020, we read: "This period has not been easy, but it has definitely been challenging and interesting, as

with other examples from other DGs.

An important decision of the President of the European Parliament, David Sassoli, has paved the way for reflection on a more advanced experiment with digitisation in the exercise of democratic functions: what I mean is an experiment not limited only to supporting the functioning of the institution, but where we get to exercise the powers of the democratic system through digitisation. This would be a significant development. We read in the preamble to President Sassoli's decision[6], "while protecting health, Parliament as a critical infrastructure of democracy in the European Union should retain its capacity to exercise its core functions as attributed to the Institution by the Treaty on European Union; information technology tools should, to the extent possible, replace physical meetings and thus contribute to enabling Parliament to exercise its core functions" and, in the operative part, "the Secretary-General shall take the measures necessary to enable remote participation to meetings of Parliament's governing bodies, committees and the plenary, without prejudice to decisions of the Bureau of the European Parliament on matters relating to the conduct of sittings." The implementation of these instructions involve the provision of advanced IT tools, which is certainly essential if the operation is to be a success. The implementation of the Presidents requests has been immediate and effective. In a Note of the Secretary General the following 18 March[7] we can read that: "With the view to ensuring the continuity of the Members' exercise of their duties related to parliamentary activity, the services of the European Parliament's administration have been asked to implement measures to facilitate the remote participation of Members in parliamentary activities in the current prolonged situation of Force Majeure where they cannot physically attend the meetings. Remote participation means being able to view and listen to proceedings, ask for the floor and intervene in the meeting. (...) Four meeting rooms have

---

it has allowed us to learn a lot about the way we work together, while continuing to provide high quality services" (Sofia Pacheco).

[6]Decision of the President of the European Parliament, CP D(2020)9886, Brussels, 9 March 2020.

[7]Der Generalsekretär, *Remote participation for Members in Parliamentary activities*, D(2020)10901, 18 March 2020.

been equipped to be operational to host parliamentary meetings (...) With this solution, both the Members participating directly from the Parliament's meeting room and those participating remotely will be able to express themselves (...) The tool also offers the possibility of remote polling. Whether this feature is used or not is a political decision." That's what can be called a frank successful reaction from the administration point of view, in such an emergency conditions.

Obviously, this is not eDemocracy as the term is understood in this study, but support for the functioning of the institution. However, it is clear that its development towards something that we can call digital democracy will depend exclusively on the rules determining how we are to operate in the new way: these rules will be a fundamental and founding element of any digital democracy. They are the essential precursor and indeed a sine qua non for the launch of any form of digital democracy. In the specific circumstance of the Covid-19 emergency, the need for specific rules for a digital vote was very clear to top management, both administrative and political, and so urgent ad hoc measures were taken. An extraordinary meeting of the Bureau was convened to adopt rules derogating from the Rules of Procedure on the basis of a proposal submitted by the Secretary General. This action was manifestly necessary and urgent in order for Parliament to adopt Commission proposals (under the ordinary legislative procedure) which were of an urgent nature and designed to deploy common European actions to counter the problems arising from Covid-19: Parliament was convened to meet in plenary session on 26 March 2020 with the aim of adopting the European Commission's proposals. The preparatory file for the Bureau meeting[8] describes precisely why, how and when it was intended to proceed so as to allow MEPs to vote remotely:

> *"In light of the current situation and the overriding public health restrictions on, inter alia, travel applicable to some Members, as well as the need for Parliament to be in a position to adopt the urgent measures proposed by the Commission as part of the EU-coordinated response to COVID-19, it is proposed that the*

[8]Technical Notes for the extraordinary meeting of the Bureau on Friday 20 March 2020, Brussels, PE 649.203/BUR.

> *Bureau supplement its 2004 Decision on rules governing voting.*
>
> *The proposal in the annex to the note from the Secretary-General seeks to allow for a temporary derogation on public health grounds, upon decision by the President, to enable the vote to take place by an alternative electronic voting procedure, with adequate safeguards to ensure that Members' votes are individual, personal and free, in line with the provisions of the Electoral act and the Members' Statute.*
>
> *In particular, Members would receive electronically, via email to their official email address, a ballot form, which would be returned, completed, from their email address to the relevant Parliament's functional mailbox. The results of all votes conducted under this temporary derogation would be recorded in the minutes of the sitting concerned. This decision would remain in force until its repeal by the Bureau, once the public health emergency has abated".*

The Bureau confirmed and adopted the proposal, by attributing to the President the full power to decide "if and when" to use the alternative method of voting[9]. The technical solution adopted was as simple as effective, that's the following[10]:

- *Where the President has decided under Article 1 that the alternative electronic voting system shall be used, the voting shall take place in accordance with the following arrangements:*
    - a) *The voting list as well as the opening time and closing time of the vote shall be published on Parliament's website. The voting list, the ballot form as well as the opening time and closing time of the vote shall be sent by electronic mail from the mailbox "plenaryvote@europarl.europa.eu" to the professional mailbox of each Member.*
    - b) *The Member shall vote by filling in and signing the ballot form on paper.*
    - c) *The Member shall send a copy of his or her ballot form, scanned or photographed in PDF, JPG or any similar stan-*

[9]Decision of the Bureau of the European Parliament of 20 March 2020 supplementing its Decision of 3 May 2004 on rules governing voting, PE 649.211/BUR

[10]Ibid. art. 2.

dard electronic format allowing for a clear and readable image, by electronic mail from his or her professional mailbox to the mailbox "plenaryvote@europarl.europa.eu".

d) *The President shall establish the result of the vote on the basis of the ballot forms which comply with the requirements of points (b) and (c) and have been received before or at the closing time mentioned in point (a).*

The two intelligent ideas underlying this approach are, firstly, maximum simplification of the voting mechanism (exchange of e-mails), which avoids the technical and legal problems associated with online voting[11], and, secondly, the temporary and exceptional nature of the action, precisely because its simplicity can only be a one-off. As I said earlier, in fact, if you want to insert online remote voting into a "normal" mechanism for the functioning of democratic powers, the rules had to be deepened and detailed[12], as well as underpinned by a much more complex technological support than a mere e-mail. However, the Plenary meeting of 26 March 2020 was a success[13] and the experience gained as a result of Covid-19 is a very useful and important starting point, should ever the European Parliament wish to move towards a systematic solution. The experience was evaluated

[11]See what I have said on this specific issue in Chapter 3.

[12]The EP, in this case, needs to revise or to complete the following body of regulations. Rule 186 of the Rules of Procedure, on the right to vote, which provides that the right to vote is a personal right and Members shall cast their votes individually and in person. Rule 187 of the Rules of Procedure, on voting, which empowers the President to decide at any time that the voting operations be carried out by means of an electronic voting system. Rule 192 of the Rules of Procedure, on the use of the electronic voting system which provides, in paragraph 1, that the Bureau shall lay down instructions determining the technical arrangements for use of the electronic voting system. The Bureau Decision of 3 May 2004 on rules governing voting, as amended, which lays down the technical arrangements for electronic voting.

[13]There were 688 MEPs participating to the vote. See: https://www.europarl.europa.eu/plenary/en/infos-details.html?id=18123&type=Flash. During the April 2020 plenary session, the number of MEPs participating in the votes (who were numerous in this case) always exceeded 680, attaining a maximum of 696, which is a remarkable figure. However, someone raised the following question: with Parliament holding its latest virtual session this week, are MEPs able adequately to represent their constituents and engage in necessary debates?

in a detailed analysis conducted by the responsible services, with an overview of the preparatory works and the running of voting procedures. The result has been considered by the Secretary General as a positive experience: "The alternative electronic voting procedure presents a valid tool to ensure the operational capacity of Parliament in the current context of public health emergency. It allows Parliament to react quickly and play its full role in the adoption of urgent measures etc.[14]". It must not be overlooked that this reasoning must also be extended to the parliamentary committees, because, as has been rightly pointed out, "there is no plenary without parliamentary committee": here too, rapid adaptation to the new situation has been crucial[15].

A considerable step forward has been done at the occasion on the Plenary meeting on 13 May 2020. As was described: "The new ITEC remote voting application ran without bugs and with excellent reactivity. In total, 695 MEPs took part in the first voting session and 687 in the second, which is a very high participation rate. We have had very few issues on the user side and most of them have been resolved instantly: we have reinforced further the capacity of the Parliament to execute its democratic mandate thanks to our technological efforts. Our priority now is to solve some small pending issues on the user side and to move forward with enriching the solution[16]". Several technical adjustments and improvements were put in place by the services concerning, inter alia, the stability of microphone and headphone

[14]Der Generalsekretär, *Assessment of the alternative electronic voting procedure at the part-session held on 26 March 2020*, D(2020)12076, 7 April 2020. Newshound, *Democracy goes on*, Edition 631, 1 April 2020, offers a narrative reconstruction of events related to the experience. This was completed later with the description of the measures on business continuity: see Newshound, *EP business continuity in times of Covid-19*, Edition 632, 15 April 2020.

[15]See Newshound, *IPOL and EXPO facing the challenge of Covid-19*, Edition 633, 22 April 2020, with its detailed reportage of how the work of parliamentary committees is continuing despite the lockdown: adjustments in record time, new organisational priorities, discussion and voting of MEPs.

[16]Internal message of the (Acting) Director General W. Petrucci on 14 May. The new solution had been tested by DG ITEC and DG PRES the week before with a series of 4 small voting sessions. The system can be used with a EP hybrid computer or with a personal device together with a SMS token.

connections as well as the visio quality. The overall stability of the system has been considerably improved[17]. The June plenary adopted the same voting system and provided for a number of enhancements including the possibility to conduct secret ballots. A total of 609 votes were held over 8 voting sessions. Overall, the voting system continued to be stable and reliable throughout the entire part-session. Members' participation in the voting sessions was very high with a maximum number of 698 – 99.1% of Members (Wednesday 16.30) – with 696 valid votes (99.7% of votes cast). In the July session, all this became "normality", the method became consolidated and the Plenary worked as if it had always operated in this way : a total of 342 votes were held, Members' participation in the voting sessions was very high, with a maximum number of 699 Members voting – 99.3% of MEPs in the first vote on Thursday; overall the participation ranged from 97% (683 Members) to 99.3% (699 Members). With regard to the September plenary session (the end-date of this analysis), the Bureau decided to apply the same system of distance voting, in parallel with the system for Members attending physically, in order to ensure the participation of Members belonging to at-risk groups and those unable to travel owing to possible restrictions[18]. Finally, the Bureau at its meeting of 14 September 2020 decided that the alternative electronic voting system is prolonged until 31 December 2020[19], while since the second plenary session in October 2020 remote participation on the part of Members has also become possible (and actually used) in the EP Liaison Offices (EPLOs) located in the Member States[20].

After the summer recess, work to adopt rules of procedure as quickly as possible accelerated and the committee responsible (AFCO) adopted its draft report in October 2020[21]. The new rules will ensure

[17]COVID-19: Remote participation facilities for Members – Note from the Secretary-General, in Technical Notes for the Meeting of the Bureau on Monday 11 May 2020, PE 650.201/BUR.

[18]See *Communication du Bureau n.6/2020*, Brussels 13 July 2020, PE 653.525/BUR.

[19]See the Bureau *Notice N° 7/2020, Brussels, 17.09.2020, PE 657.899/BUR*

[20]See ITEC Newsletter October 2020, which mentions "formidable inter-DG cooperation".

[21]AFCO started to work on this already in May 2020 and the EP Conference of Presidents discussed the matter in September. At the time when this report

that Parliament will have provisions in place to facilitate its functioning in extraordinary circumstances, taking into account the lessons learnt from the COVID-19 health crisis. As explained in detail in a press release from that committee: "the proposed changes envision the activation of emergency measures by the President, with consent from the Conference of Presidents, for the entirety or part of Parliament's work. If it is deemed necessary, including when Parliament's political balance is disturbed, such measures may include the postponement, displacement or remote organisation of activities. Extraordinary measures will have to be activated for a specific amount of time and only for events that are exceptional, unforeseeable, and outside Parliament's control. Further, MEPs will be able to reverse these decisions by simple majority in Parliament's plenary sessions. Attention was also given to ensuring that MEPs can participate equally, freely and in their native language (to the greatest possible extent), and through secure electronic systems[22]".

Although it may seem somewhat ponderous, it is very useful to mention the purely technical aspects, because that is where the solution lies. DG ITEC explained in detail how it was possible to resolve the problem: "The new ?Plenary-voting' application makes a bridge between two existing applications; namely ALV, the application that manages the lists of votes, and ACTES, which manages the results of votes. The Plenary-voting app was added as a module of ACTES in order to benefit from the existing infrastructure. To use the new system, Members can connect from anywhere with a hybrid computer provided by the European Parliament or via a personal device using a physical or SMS token. From the technology side, European Parliament standards (such as HTML5, CSS and JavaScript) were used for the development of the applications. The system is accessible from the most popular browsers (Edge, Chrome, Firefox, Safari, Internet Explorer and Opera). As it is accessible from everywhere, there was a focus on the reactivity of the application so that bandwidth usage is as low as possible. Moreover, all Members, including those

went to press, the Plenary had not yet expressed its view.

[22]AFCO Press Releases 13-10-2020 (https://www.europarl.europa.eu/news/en/press-room/20201012IPR89120/)

present in Parliament's premises, vote in the same way. When the President opens the vote, Members receive a link to an online ballot form, which is accessible for the duration of the voting time. Once Members finalise their vote on the application, they receive an email with a ballot paper in PDF format, pre-filled with their votes, which they must print, sign, scan and send back for their votes to be taken into account[23]".

The deployment of such a complex, multilingual solution would normally have taken several months if not years. In view of the urgent need and on request by the Secretary-General, the responsible services in DG LINC speeded up the required specific technical tests to allow for the immediate deployment of multilingual remote participation tools for Members. From 19 March until 4 September 2020, the remote meeting system was used for over 700 meetings with almost 65 000 participants in total: 12 meeting rooms were equipped with the system, 8 rooms are used regularly and 6 meetings with up to 9 languages were organised in parallel on a regular basis. 1 000 connections were possible at the same time in parallel meetings. Since 7 September 2020 it was possible to organise meetings with a total of 12 languages in parallel in 2 meeting rooms[24]. A special effort was deployed for the parliamentary committees activities: staff in DG IPOL and DG EXPO continued to support the work of MEPs. In a publication specifically dealing with this, we can read: "irrespective of their physical location, MEPs continue holding debates and taking decisions to ensure the EU can adopt the measures needed to address the COVID-19 crisis, to ensure the benefit of all EU citizens and beyond, establish a recovery plan and relaunch the economy. Due to these unprecedented circumstances, several meeting rooms were equipped with new videoconference facilities, allowing remote meetings to be held with the availability of simultaneous interpretation[25]".

In order to ensure a solid, structural future for this process of in-

---

[23]DG ITEC Newsletter, 28 May 2020.

[24]See *Technical Notes for the meeting of the Bureau on Monday, 14 September 2020, PE 653.583/BUR, cit.*

[25]See DG IPOL-DG EXPO, *The European parliamentary committees' response to COVID-19. Ensuring the continuation of the legislative and democratic life of the European Union. An Overview*, Brussels, July 2020.

novation, the EPA must implement many of the ongoing, interrelated projects, but there are two that are preliminary in the sense that they are essential for the success of the other projects and the process of innovation we have just described: they are, on the one hand, "Full implementation of eParliament" (SEF 2017-19) and on the other hand "From eParliament to eLegislate" (SEF 2019-21). The two projects are integrated. The final report on the implementation of the first project[26] states that it is delayed and more precisely "far from being completed", which is a dangerous handicap because of its structural and inter-service character, in so far as it aims to support the "core" activity of Parliament: completion of this project is urgent also because it is linked to the second. "From eParliament to eLegislate" constitutes, indeed, an extension and development of the first, with precise objectives: projects included in eParliament should cover all aspects of the legislative chain; digitalisation should be extended to other parliamentary processes such as the creation of voting lists or committee agendas; there should be an inter-institutional approach for business and IT interoperability across the Institutions, and the visibility of Parliament's legislative work should be increased through digitalisation[27]. Around these technical solutions revolve many other projects which depend on them.

The Covid-19 emergency showed the key role of the administration, in this case of EPA: then, it is important, at the end of my analysis, to base myself again on the political impetus of the Plenary by recalling Parliament's resolution on EU eGovernment[28]. Here, in fact, the European Parliament speaks directly and explicitly about administration: just at the beginning of the resolution we read that "the modernisation strategies of public administrations must be adapted to a changing environment enabling the transformation to digital government" (para. A), while a little further on, the Plenary states that "public administrations should be open, transparent, efficient

[26] See the aforementioned *Strategic Execution Framework. For the Administration of the European Parliament 2017-2019*, Conclusion SEF 2017 2019, Edition June 2019.

[27] See the aforementioned *Strategic Execution Framework 2019-2021*, http://www.sef.ep.parl.union.eu/sef/cycles/2/home, web page 9

[28] Resolution of 16 May 2017, cited in Chapter 2.

and inclusive" (para. 2). Let us therefore see how Parliament's administration responds in practice and structurally to these demands, in addition to what I have told about Covid-19 situation.

To do so and to conclude this report with a focus on operational aspects, the analysis conducted so far allows me to state with certainty that, *as things stand today, "the EPA's operational approach to eDemocracy" is very rich, very broad and very solid.* In fact, there are many projects which have already been implemented, many under way, and many ideas to be developed in the future. Here are those that I have identified in the course of the analysis:

- eCommittee
- eMeeting
- Drafting Support Tool
- AT4AM
- Digital Signature
- ICT services for constituency offices
- XML, metadata and indexing
- eVote
- Citizens' Portal & Citizens' App
- Consultation of National Parliament on implementation
- Petitions and Citizens' Enquiries review
- EP's stakeholder dialogue
- URBIS. Digital HUB for consultation
- Online polling on priorities
- My House of European History (1)
- Citizens' APP go local
- Data Driven Communication
- Parliament Open Data
- Hub with National Parliaments on Democracy Support Activities
- Partnership with Local Governmental Organisations
- Partnership with Regional Governmental Organisations
- Partnership with National Parliaments on Implementation
- Identifying Expectations Gaps
- Multiplier Networks Civil Society
- My House of European History (2)

- Youth Engagement
- Cyber-Security and Cyber Defence
- Establishing a regular system of information sharing on EU policy work
- Automated digital "sentiment" analysis of publicly available material
- Developing and promoting an electronic platform to collect contributions
- Dialogue initiatives, based on online participation
- Challenging election manipulation made by modern technologies
- Action plan against disinformation
- Organising citizens' participation in the Conference on the Future of Europe
- European cloud and data infrastructure
- Joint Cybersecurity Unit
- European Cybersecurity Competence Centres
- Support for other parliaments
- Parliamentary open data
- Introducing artificial intelligence for services
- Observatory on Artificial Intelligence.

To add more proposals would be absurd (in the sense of unreasonable), indeed it would be a serious political and management error. The EPA must now concentrate on making all this a normal reality. In order to achieve this, the only suggestion that can be put forward is to structure the sector organisationally so as to make it uniform: for example, by means of a transversal Steering Working Group, coordinated at the level of the Secretary General's Cabinet, while making it a corporate goal: in this way it will be possible to construct what the Secretary General has called a "multisector approach". I consider that the Steering Working Group (SWG) could focus on the following activities.

First, I believe that the SWG should check whether the EPA is technically equipped to carry out all the eDemocracy related projects as listed above. This first aspect is obviously extremely delicate because it constitutes the infrastructural support of the whole construction: being technically equipped means having all the conditions, means, tools, equipment and knowledge to develop, produce and realise all the projects planned. In this context, in addition to verifying that the technological capabilities exist and work, the SWG should in my opinion focus on the management of open data, including the use of the semantic web and the ad hoc use of AI: open data is the basis and a precondition for the functioning of eDemocracy tools.

Secondly, the SWG should take seriously into account something which is pointed out in an EPRS document[29]: online platforms are designed to have an impact; yet, many people reported poorly designed websites with unnecessarily complex procedures and bad timing, with the result that they are still, for the most part, time-consuming and somewhat of a disappointment for citizens. The EPRS document goes on to say that the question is how to redesign existing participatory procedures using captivating, attractive formats[30]. Moreover, ICTs are essentially designed to foster contacts between citizen users or commercial practices and very little or nothing is designed for the needs of administrations: this makes it difficult for the EPA to create and develop new applications. It also makes the necessary role of moderator of the communities participating in the platforms created by the EPA difficult: the operating mechanisms of the platforms, for those who participate and for those who moderate, must be well defined and constantly adapted.

Thirdly, the SWG should prepare a map of the "risks" associated with the overall activity of eDemocracy instruments. As I said somewhat earlier, cybersecurity and data protection are crucially important for the robustness of the system and hence must be constantly monitored. But there are other "risks" that need to be taken

[29]EPRS, *Ten issues to watch in 2020*, authored by É. Bassot, January 2020, PE 646.116.

[30]ibid., pp. 10-11. The item is analysed broadly and in depth in G. Sgueo, *"Regulatory Gaming". A look into European Union's attempts to engage citizens with playful design*, in A. Alemanno, J. Organ, Democratic Participation in a Citizen's Europe: What Next for the EU?, Routledge, Abington, 2020 (in preparation). The author shows how EU institutions constantly seek to enhance and increase interaction with stakeholders through experimental efforts which have been intensified over the last decade.

into account in order to guarantee correct functioning of the various eDemocracy tools: in particular, so as to make sure that those tools are genuinely (internally as well as externally) used in a widespread way, i.e. that they are not dominated by organised groups. In this sense, the SWG should put everything in place in order to make the opportunities created by the EPA known and understood, but at the same time it could also pay attention to the problem of those who for various reasons could be excluded from participation.

Fourthly, the SWG could check with the responsible services that vocational training does take the eDemocracy process into account. Vocational training does a great job in supporting middle management and staff so that they apprehend the latest innovations in IT, but it would also seem necessary to "explain" these technological innovations and situate them in the general and strategic context. This point is closely linked to the more general objective of reducing inequality in technological literacy within the institution, on the part of both Members and staff, so that there is the same opportunity for all to use the tools of eDemocracy.

Fifthly, the SWG could also be charged with analysing the "accelerated" experience made under the pressure of the Covid-19 emergency, obviously within the confines of the subject of this study: it would therefore be a matter, on the one hand, of analysing the effects of the acceleration process and, on the other, of verifying which new instruments can be used to enrich the eDemocracy system within the European Parliament.

Lastly, but in point of fact this is a preventive aspect, in coordinating the activities connected with the different projects, the SWG should make provision for incorporation by homogeneous areas and for identifying priorities in the implementation process. Manifestly, this exercise, aimed at building systematic governance for the eDemocracy model within the European Parliament, has consequences for the way the administration works. The EPA has a solid methodological basis, which is under constant development: it will be the task of the SWG to ascertain how the new requirements should fit into the current methodological project and what adaptations should be made.

As I mentioned at the beginning of this report (see the Scope), the administration is first and foremost at the service of the activity of the Members and the fulfilment of the institution's tasks: it is the duty of the EPA, therefore, to ensure that everything that has been analysed and described here is fully directed towards this objective. It is the prerogative of Parliament, as the major political institution representing citizens, to ensure that actions in support of democracy through digitisation are implemented: building people's trust in technology and digital transformation, regulating how companies collect and use data, improving transparency and access to documents, online consultation and participation of citizens, and so on with many others. From the institution's point of view, until yesterday the use of technology could be seen as an opportunity to make activities more efficient and modern, but today this has clearly become an unavoidable necessity.

Chapter 8

Closing

Ruf, Beruf und Sache (Max Weber).

In sum, much has been done and much needs to be done following the same methodological and teleological approach: but who should do it? As Max Weber explained in a way that has never been unsurpassed, the three essential subjects/protagonists are: science/technology, the political sphere and the administration[1]. Weber understood perfectly where we were going a century ago and his analysis is altogether suited to the current situation, specifically to our question of eDemocracy, a fortiori in the context of the Covid-19 emergency: in fact, the three protagonists in question are hard at work, as I showed in the preceding pages. This is why the attention recently paid to Max Weber by one of the greatest philosophers of our time, Massimo Cacciari, was very appropriate and timely. His essay on "*geistige Arbeit*"[2] prompted me to close this report by recalling Max Weber, whose works have been my constant reference and, through certain epistemic ideas, cast light on what we have been analysing in

[1] M. Weber, *The Vocation Lectures* (Edited and with an Introduction by D. Owen and T.B. Strong, Translation by R. Livingstone), Hackett, Indianapolis/Cambridge, 2004: this book brings together the celebrated lectures given by Max Weber in Vienna (1917-1919) on "*Wissenschaft als Beruf*" and "*Politik als Beruf*".

[2] M. Cacciari, *Il lavoro dello spirito. Saggio su Max Weber*, Adelphi, Milano, 2020.

this report. Weber explains that in modern times the main dialectic, which in truth is a relationship that tends to be conflictual, is between science/technology and the political sphere: in both cases, Weber said, evolution would lead to their professionalisation, to the disenchantment of the world, risking a separation that will have to be reconciled. On the one hand, there is science/technology concentrated on its subject-matter (Sache) in complete autonomy and with its tendency to be hegemonic; on the other hand, there is the political sphere, which has to come to terms with science/technology, but must be able to take the most appropriate decisions, that is to say, must be able to decide having regard to all the elements necessary for the government of society and not only the subject-matter of science. This is exactly what we are experiencing today in general terms with technological progress, which tends to be hegemonic and separated from the political sphere, while the latter tries to bring everything back together within the framework of a global governance of society: the case of eDemocracy is certainly one of the most important aspects of this phenomenon and this has been accentuated by Covid-19.

The question is: where is the factor of possible reconciliation to be found? The philosopher Massimo Cacciari, reconstructing Weber's thought, tells us: "Without a technical-bureaucratic apparatus, without organisation, without skills, politics is not a profession, and will therefore necessarily be ineffective in governing a world dominated by technical/scientific powers. A political sphere which does not want or is unable to structure itself professionally internally and equip itself as a whole with powerful administrative/bureaucratic structures will simply be opting for impotence"[3].

A Weberian echo in this sense bounced up in the speech that President Sassoli gave to Parliament's staff to mark Innovation Day: Sassoli, after saying how proud he was of how Parliament's administration had worked and acted in the Covid-19 emergency situation, stated that the political level and the administration were closely linked and had to act in synergy. This event was held on 11 September 2020 in an atmosphere still characterised by the emergency: indeed, the theme chosen referred to the on-going emergency experience, the

[3]ibid., pp. 55-56.

event being entirely devoted to teleworking[4], with an eye to the near future. Secretary General Klaus Welle stressed that from an administration working mainly on-site, Parliament had moved close to full teleworking almost overnight. Remote working methods and collaborative tools had been deployed to ensure the best possible working conditions for Members and staff. According to Welle, comforted by the results of an extensive survey that showed a positive assessment by the vast majority of the staff[5], this experience can be transformed from a crisis into an opportunity by avoiding a return to the *statu quo ante*. It is very interesting to note the evolution of the approach to teleworking, to which I have already dedicated some passages in the previous pages: initially considered a tool to reconcile family life and working life, it was then enriched (in the same context) by the idea that it would also promote efficiency, then with Covid-19 it appeared as a necessary tool to cope with the emergency, and finally it became a possible structural solution to the organisation of work. This evolution concerns the whole world of work and not only public administrations, provided that the problems I mentioned above are resolved (within a new paradigm): mediocre performance, difficulties in time management, loss of team spirit, and isolation[6].

Indeed, in September 2020, Parliament's reflection on the issues of democracy, the impact of the health emergency and the role of technology in this context became extremely focused through the organisation of a series of seminars as part of Democracy Week[7]. This event unfolded in the knowledge that "the actions of today will shape the world of tomorrow"; for that reason, in all meetings the objective was to focus on "what we can do" to strengthen democracy and democratic

---

[4]5th Management Innovation Day: Making teleworking a success, Brussels, 11 September 2020.

[5]The Future of Teleworking-Survey, report presented by Andrea Mraz-Androvicova.

[6]See in particular the first part of the chapter, Conclusions.

[7]International Democracy Week, a series of high-level events and workshops on global democracy and the pandemic, taking place online from 14 to 17 September, organised by the International Institute for Democracy and Electoral Assistance, the European Endowment for Democracy, the European Partnership for Democracy, the European Network of Political Foundations, and Carnegie Europe, in partnership with the European Parliament.

innovation. In my opinion, one of the most acute observations made during Democracy Week is that the health crisis has shown (worldwide) how easy it is to impose restrictions on the democratic system and its mechanisms of checks and balances; but it has also shown the high degree of resilience of democratic institutions: this is truly an important observation. More specifically on our theme, eDemocracy, the event highlighted that "the COVID-19 crisis has pushed digitalisation to the top of the EU's agenda, with tech companies developing contact tracing apps and countering the infodemic, while civic tech groups have developed tech solutions to mitigate the crisis. This is a critical moment for the EU's digital future, with the opportunity for policies to centre around how citizens and their elected representatives can regain control over the digital space: this means to explore how the trends in digital technologies and opportunities in digital policy interact with the trend of autocratisation in Europe and around the world." A theme that involves answering many of the issues raised in Democracy Week: "How has the Covid-19 pandemic accelerated and intensified some of the trends in digital technologies? How are some of these trends in conflict with democratic principles? How has this affected the already fragile state of European democracy? How can digital technologies and digital policy be leveraged to strengthen democracy in Europe and in EU external action?"

A first contribution to finding an answer to these questions came in the same week from the speech on the "State of the Union" made to Parliament by the President of the European Commission, Ursula von der Leyen (VdL), on 16 September 2020[8]. Addressing Members of Parliament, VdL urged them to imagine for a moment life in this pandemic without digital in our lives: it enabled companies (she said) to sell their products, factories to keep running and government to deliver crucial public services from afar. According to VdL we saw years' worth of digital innovation and transformation in the space of a few weeks, we are reaching the limits of the things we can do in an analogue way: and this great acceleration is just beginning. In the view of VdL we need a common plan for digital Europe with clearly defined goals for 2030, such as for connectivity, skills and digital public

[8]https://ec.europa.eu/commission/presscorner/detail/en/SPEECH_20_1655

services and we need to follow clear principles: the right to privacy and connectivity, freedom of speech, free flow of data and cybersecurity. There are three areas on which VdL believes we need to focus: data, artificial intelligence and infrastructure, which must make what VdL called "Europe's Digital Decade".

And it was precisely digital transformation that was the theme of Parliament's Bureau Away Days, held on 24 and 25 September 2020 in Brussels. The subjects dealt with were varied: teleworking and related themes such as hybrid events and remote meeting capacities[9]; the experience of visitor centres[10]; the future of parliamentarism[11]. In his introduction to the proceedings, President Sassoli recalled that the emergency had imposed decisions never taken or imagined before, in order to guarantee the democratic control that is the nature of parliaments and which is increasingly necessary. The whole of the ensuing debate highlighted the European Parliament's great capacity for innovation, both politically and administratively; in general it was stressed that there is no going back from the process of digital transformation, but bearing in mind that what is involved is factors of integration and the strengthening of normal presential work which remains essential for democracy by virtue of the exchanges of opinions and reflections that it allows. In order to strike a proper balance between physical and remote presence it is also necessary to take action with regard to Parliament's Rules of Procedure: during the emergency, decisions were taken using the leeway allowed by the rules in force, but the debate has shown that new elements had to be introduced in to those rules so as to allow the necessary great flexibility[12]. The key element that emerged clearly from the debate at Parliament's Bureau seminar in September 2020 is that all this is

[9]Success factors for teleworking: enabling tools and digital workflows, Introduction by K. Dobrev; Towards hybrid events, Introduction by O. Karas and K. Barley; Remote meeting capacities: from challenge to reality, Introduction by N. Beer.

[10]Europa Experience Centres. Implementation and timeline, Introduction by R. Wieland.

[11]At the service of the citizens. The future of Parliamentarism, Introduction by P. Silva Pereira.

[12]As we saw in the previous chapter, the Constitutional Affairs Committee adopted a draft report the month after the debate at the Bureau's seminar.

not a simple functional approach which allows the machine to move forward even in an emergency. All of this, in truth, is something that influences the future of parliamentary democracy: combining the use of digital technologies with the proper functioning of democratic institutions, Parliament in our specific case, is a work of the highest sensitivity.

The officials of the European Parliament are highly qualified and fit for purpose; to a very large extent indeed, they have the characteristics indicated by Max Weber: they feel called (*Ruf*) to their work, which they seek to carry out with the utmost integrity in their vocation (*Beruf*), in order to contribute to that "system of freedom" which European thought has been trying to establish for millennia (*ἁρχή*). This can be achieved only in the context of democracy, working free from *δόξα* or dogma, exclusively in the responsible defence of values. This is precisely the quintessentially noble role which the European Parliament Administration plays and will have to play in the development of eDemocracy.

References

The texts listed below were consulted in order to develop the analysis of this work and are explicitly mentioned in the footnotes: in so far as they are books, essays, studies, documents of the European Parliament and other European institutions, web pages, and resolutions of the Plenary, they are listed in the order in which they are mentioned in the report; other sources, meetings and seminars are listed in chronological order.

BIBLIOGRAPHY

E. Fawcett, *Liberalism. The Life of an Idea*, Princeton University Press, Oxford, 2019.

Y.N. Harari, *The World after coronavirus*, in Financial Times, March 20, 2020.

IPU-Centre for Innovation in Parliament, *Parliamentary Responses to Coronavirus*, Live Document, updated April 2020.

Commonwealth Parliamentary Association, Covid-19. *Delivering Parliamentary Democracy*, London, April 2020

D. Runciman, *Così finisce la democrazia. Paradossi, presente e futuro di un'istituzione imperfetta*, Bollati Boringhieri, Torino, 2019.

N. Baverez, *L'alerte démocratique*, L'Observatoire, Paris, 2020.

S. Levitsky and D. Ziblatt, *How Democracies Die*, Crown, New York, 2018.

G. Sartori, *Democrazia e definizioni*, Il Mulino, Bologna, 1957.

I. Kershaw, *Roller coaster: Europe 1950-2017*, Penguin UK, London, 2018.

V. E. Parsi, *Titanic. Il naufragio dell'ordine liberale*, Il Mulino, Bologna, 2018

E. Luce, *The Retreat of Western Liberalism*, Little, Brown, London, 2017.

J. Stiglitz, *People, Power, and Profits*, Penguin, London, 2019.

T. Piketty, *Capital et idéologie*, Seuil, Paris, 2019.

M. Vargas Llosa, *La corrección política es enemiga de la libertad*, El País semanal, Entrevista, 25.2.2018.

M. Vargas Llosa, *La llamada de la tribu*, Alfaguara, Barcelona, 2018.

F. Fukuyama, *Identity. The Demand for Dignity and the Politics of Resentment*, Edizioni Farrar Straus and Giroux, New York, 2018.

N. Urbinati (ed.), Introduction, in *Thinking democracy now. Between Innovation and Regression*, Feltrinelli Editore, Milano, 2019

N. Urbinati, *Io, il popolo. Come il populismo trasforma la democrazia*, il Mulino, Bologna, 2020

J. Lacroix - J.Y. Pranchère, *Les droits de l'homme rendent-ils idiots?*, Editions Seuil, Paris, 2019.

D. Innerarity, *Una teoría de la democracia compleja. Gobernar en el siglo XXI*, Galaxia Gutenberg, Barcelona, 2020.

M. J. Martinez Iglesias, *The Accidental Democracy: A European Model, in Garben-Govaere-Nemitz (ed.), Critical Reflections on Constitutional Democracy in the European Union*, Hart Publishing, Oxford, 2019

R. Dahrendorf, Erasmiani. *Gli intellettuali alla prova del totalitarismo*, Laterza, Roma-Bari, 2007.

L. Floridi, *Il verde e il blu*, Raffaello Cortina Editore, Milano, 2020

M. Telò, *L'Europa potenza civile*, Laterza, Roma-Bari, 2004.

P. Rossel and M. Finger, "Conceptualizing e-Governance" Management, in ICEGOV07 Proceedings of the 1st international conference on Theory and practice of electronic governance, Macao, Chine, 2007, p. 399-407.

A. Macintosh, "*Characterizing E-Participation in Policy-Making*", in Proceedings of the 37th Annual Hawaii International Conference on System Sciences (HICSS'04), January 05 - 08, 2004.

L. Violante, *Rifondare la democrazia nella società digitale*, in Storia e Memoria, n. 1/2020, p. 123 s.

S. Cassese, *Il popolo e i suoi rappresentanti*, Edizioni di Storia e Letteratura, Roma, 2019.

F. Foer, *I nuovi poteri forti come Google, Apple, Facebook e Amazon pensano per noi*, Longanesi, Milano, 2018

G. Lovink, *Nichilismo digitale. L'altra faccia delle piattaforme*, EGEA - Bocconi Editore, Milano, 2019

S. Zuboff, *Il capitalismo della sorveglianza*, Luiss University Press, Roma, 2019.

M. Delmastro – A. Nicita, *Big Data – Come stanno cambiando il nostro mondo* Il Mulino, Bologna, 2019

COM(2020)67 final, *Shaping Europe's Digital Future*, Brussels 19.02.2020.

Presidency of the Council of the European Union, *Conference on the Future of Europe*, AG32 INST120, Brussels, 24 June 2020

European Commission, DG CONNECT, *Digital Economy and Society Index*, Report 2020, online

European Commission, *Recovery Plan for Europe*, online

COM (2018) 237 final, L'intelligence artificielle pour l'Europe and COM (2018) 795 final, Coordinated Plan on Artificial Intelligence.

Independent High Level Expert Group on Artificial Intelligence, *Ethics Guidelines for Trustworthy AI*, Document made public on 8 April 2019

European Commission, *White Paper on Artificial Intelligence – A European approach to excellence and trust*, Brussels, 19.2.2020, COM(2020) 65 final.

European Commission, *Guidance on Apps supporting the fight against COVID 19 pandemic in relation to data protection*, Brussels, 16.4.2020, C(2020) 2523 final.

EC Joint Research Centre, *Understanding our political nature*, EUR 29783EN, Luxembourg, 2019.

EDPS Ethics Advisory Group, Towards a digital ethics, Report 2018, European Union, Brussels, 2018.

EDPS, *Outcome of own-initiative investigation into EU institutions' use of Microsoft products and services*, Brussels, 2 July 2020

G. Sgueo, *"Regulatory Gaming". A look into European Union's attempts to engage citizens with playful design*, in A. Alemanno, J. Organ, Democratic Participation in a Citizen's Europe: What Next for the EU?, Routledge, Abington, 2020 (in preparation).

R. D'Apolito and A. Fratini, *Smart Working facile (E non solo)*, FineAdvisors, published by Amazon Poland, 2020

M. Weber, *The Vocation Lectures* (Edited and with an Introduction by D. Owen and T.B. Strong, Translation by R. Livingstone), Hackett, Indianapolis/Cambridge, 2004

M. Cacciari, *Il lavoro dello spirito. Saggio su Max Weber*, Adelphi, Milano, 2020

G. Vilella, *Being European*, (Foreword by Klaus Welle), Nomos, Baden-Baden, 2017, especially at pp.101-105.

G. Vilella, *Working methods of the European Parliament Administration. A reflection paper, Brussels, 1st July 2019*

EP DOCUMENTS

EPRS, *Protecting the rule of law in the EU. Existing mechanisms and possible improvements*, authored by R. Manko, November 2019, PE 642.280

EPRS/STOA, *Prospects for e-democracy in Europe*, February 2018, PE 603.213, under the responsibility of G. Quaglio and T. Karapiperis

EPRS, *Digital democracy. Is the future of civic engagement online?*, authored by G. Sgueo, February 2020, PE 646.161.

EPRS, *The practice of democracy. A selection of civic engagement initiatives*, authored by G. Sgueo, June 2020, PE 651.970

EPRS, *Covid-19's impact on human rights outside the EU*, authored by I. Zamfir, PE 649.365, April 2020.

European Parliament resolution of 17 April 2020 on EU coordinated action to combat the COVID-19 pandemic and its consequences, P9_TA-PROV(2020)0054

EPRS, *Parliaments in emergency mode How Member States' parliaments are continuing with business during the pandemic*, authored by M. Díaz Crego and R. Ma.ko, PE 649.396, April 2020

D. M. Sassoli, *President's Speech at the European Council*, Brussels 17 October 2019 (PDF).

The European Parliament 2025 - Preparing for complexity, Brussels, January 2012

MEP 2025 – Preparing the Future Work Environment for Members of the European Parliament, Brussels, March 2012

European Parliament resolution 16 March 2017 on *eDemocracy in the EU: potential and challenges* P8_TA(2017)095.

European Parliament resolution of 16 May 2017 on the EU eGovernment Action Plan 2016-2020, P8_TA(2017)0205

European Parliament resolution of 10 March 2016 on '*Towards a thriving data-driven economy*', P8_ TA(2016)0089

European Parliament resolution of 28 April 2016 on *public access to documents* (Rule 116(7)) for the years 2014-2015, P8_TA(2016)0202

European Parliament resolution of 2 March 2017 on *the implementation of Council Regulation (EU) No 390/2014 of 14 April 2014 establishing the Europe for Citizens' programme* for the period 2014-2020, P8_TA(2017)0063

European Parliament resolution of 31 May 2018 on the implementation of the EU Youth Strategy, P8_ TA(2018)0240

European Parliament legislative resolution of 12 March 2019 on *the proposal for a regulation of the European Parliament and of the Council on the European citizens' initiative*, P8_TA(2019)0153

European Parliament Resolution of 13 February 2019 on the state of the debate on the future of Europe, P8_TA(2019)0098

European Parliament resolution of 15 January 2020 on the European Parliament's position on the Conference on the Future of Europe, P9_TA-PROV(2020)0010

Regulation (EU) 2016/679 of the European Parliament and of the Council of 27 April 2016 on the protection of natural persons with regard to the processing of personal data and on the free movement of such data, and repealing Directive 95/46/EC, OJ L 119, 4.5.2016,

Directive (EU) 2016/680 of the European Parliament and of the Council of 27 April 2016 on the protection of natural persons with regard to the processing of personal data by competent authorities for the purposes of the prevention, investigation, detection or prosecution of criminal offences or the execution of criminal penalties, and on the free movement of such data, and repealing Council Framework Decision 2008/977/JHA, OJ L 119, 4.5.2016.

European Parliament resolution of 25 October 2018 on the use of Facebook users' data by Cambridge Analytica and the impact on data protection, P8_TA(2018)0433.

European Parliament resolution of 13 June 2018 on cyber defence, P8_TA(2018)0258

Regulation (EU) 2019/881 of the European Parliament and of the Council of 17 April 2019 on ENISA (the European Union Agency for Cybersecurity) and on information and communications technology cybersecurity certification and repealing Regulation (EU) No 526/2013, OJ L 151, 7.6.2019, p. 15.

EPRS, *The von der Leyen Commission's priorities for 2019-2024*, authored by É. Bassot, January 2020, PE 646.148

European Parliament, *Commitments made at the hearings of the Commissioners-designate*, Brussels, November 2019

European Parliament resolution of 16 February 2017 with *recommendations to the Commission on Civil Law Rules on Robotics*, P8-TA (2017) 0051 repealing Regulation (EU) No 526/2013, OJ L 151, 7.6.2019.

S. Kotanidis, *Preparing the Conference on the Future of Europe*, EPRS, December 2019, PE 644.202

Potential and Challenges of e-participation in the European Union, authored by E. Lironi (ECAS) for the IPOL Policy Department "C", May 2016, PE 556.949

EPRS, Next Generation EU. A European instrument to counter the impact of coronavirus pandemic, authored by A. D'Alfonso, July, PE 652.000

EPRS, eGovernment, authored by R. Davies, September 2015, PE 565.890

Innovative working in the European Parliament. A Guide, Brussels, November 2016

Strategic Execution Framework. For the Administration of the European Parliament 2017-2019, Conclusion SEF 2017-2019, Edition June 2019

Taking the Pulse. A Strategic Execution Framework for the European Union in the making (K. Welle, the Editor; A. Worum, Responsible), Brussels, European Parliament, December 2019

EPRS, *Ideas Papers for the Management Innovation Day 2020*, Brussels, European Parliament, December 2019

EPRS, *How digital technology is easing the burden of confinement*, authored by M. Negreiro, May 2020, PE 651.927

Information and Communication Technology (ICT) in the European Parliament: Strategic orientations 2019-2021, authored by W. Petrucci, with the agreement of the Secretary General, D(2019)34304, October 2019.

Strategic Execution Framework 2019-2021, http://www.sef.ep.parl.union.eu/sef/cycles/2/home

IPOL, *Role of the European Parliament in promoting the use of independent expertise in the legislative process*, authored by Mariusz Maciejewski, January 2019, PE 626.085.

EPRS-STOA, *Regulating disinformation with artificial intelligence*, March 2019, PE 624.279

DG IPOL, *The White Paper on Artificial Intelligence*, authored by M. Ciucci and F. Gouardères, PE 648.773 – April 2020

DG IPOL-DG EXPO, *The European parliamentary committees' response to COVID-19. Ensuring the continuation of the legislative and democratic life of the European Union. An Overview*, Brussels, July 2020

EPRS-STOA, *Roundtable on Digital Sovereign Identity*, 11 June 2020, Webex meeting

EPRS, *Access to e-sources while you are teleworking*, 8 April 2020.

DG ITEC, *Teleworking tools: the essentials*, 31 March 2020

Decision of the President of the European Parliament, CP D(2020)9886, Brussels, 9 March 2020.

Der Generalsekretär, *Remote participation for Members in Parliamentary activities*, D(2020)10901, 18 March 2020.

Technical Notes for the extraordinary meeting of the BUREAU on Friday 20 March 2020, Brussels, PE 649.203/BUR

Technical Notes for the meeting of the Bureau on Monday, 6 July 2020, PE 650.252/BUR

Communication du Bureau n.6/2020, Brussels 13 July 2020, PE 653.525/BUR

Decision of the Bureau of the European Parliament of 20 March 2020 supplementing its Decision of 3 May 2004 on rules governing voting, PE 649.211/BUR

Der Generalsekretär, Assessment of the alternative electronic voting procedure at the part-session held on 26 March 2020, D(2020)12076, 7 April 2020.

COVID-19: Remote participation facilities for Members – Note from the Secretary-General, in Technical Notes for the Meeting of the Bureau on Monday 11 May 2020, PE 650.201/BUR.

Bureau Notice N° 6/2020, Brussels, 13 July 2020, PE 653.525/BUR

Bureau Notice N° 7/2020, Brussels, 17.09.2020, PE 657.899/BUR

Technical Notes for the meeting of the Bureau on Monday, 14 September 2020, PE 653.583/BUR

EPRS, *Ten issues to watch in 2020*, authored by É. Bassot, January 2020, PE 646.116

SITOGRAPHY

https://ec.europa.eu/commission/presscorner/detail/en/SPEECH_19_4230

https://www.government.nl/documents/diplomatic-statements/2020/04/01/statement-by-belgium-denmark-finland-france-germany-greece-ireland-italy-luxembourg-the-netherlandsportugal-spain-sweden

https://publicadministration.un.org/egovkb/en-us/About/UNeGovDD-Framework#whatis

http://portal.oas.org/Portal/Sector/SAP/DepartamentoparalaGestiónPúblicaEfectiva/NPA/SobreProgramadeeGobierno/tabid/811/Default.aspx?language=en-us

https://en.wikipedia.org/wiki/E-government

https://en.wikipedia.org/wiki/E-governance

https://www.igi-global.com/dictionary/democracy/8663

http://e-consultation.org/gide/index.php/E-consultation

https://en.wikipedia.org/wiki/E-participation

https://www.igi-global.com/dictionary/indicators-measures-government/8868

https://www.citizenlab.co/blog

https://www.igi-global.com/dictionary/experimental-deliberation-taiwan/8673

https://www.igi-global.com/dictionary/smart-city-governance/42406

http://www.businessdictionary.com/definition/electronic-information-system.html

https://www.collinsdictionary.com/dictionary/english/e-voting

https://www.e-voting.cc/en/it-elections/definitions/

https://en.wikipedia.org/wiki/Electronic_voting

https://www.europarl.europa.eu/plenary/en/infos-details.html?id=18123&type=Flash

https://ec.europa.eu/commission/presscorner/detail/en/SPEECH_20_1655

https://www.europarl.europa.eu/news/en/press-room/20201012IPR89120

OTHER SOURCES

Corriere della Sera, 3 February 2015

Corriere della Sera, 8 July 2019

Corriere della Sera, 23 August 2019

POLITICO Brussels Playbook, 16 February 2020

POLITICO Brussels Playbook, 17 February 2020

Le Soir, 18 February 2020

Corriere della Sera, 20 February 2020

Financial Times, 20 March 2020

Corriere della Sera, 23 March 2020.

Corriere della Sera, 25 March 2020.

Le Soir, 26 March 2020.

Le Figaro, 1 April 2020

Newshound, Edition 631, 1 April 2020

POLITICO Brussels Playbook, 3 April 2020

Corriere della Sera, 6 April 2020

POLITICO Brussels Playbook, 10 April 2020

Newshound, Edition 632, 15 April 2020

Financial Times, 16 April 2020.

Le Figaro, 17 April 2020

Newshound, Edition 633, 22 April 2020

POLITICO, Brussels Playbook, 30 April 2020

DG ITEC Newsletter, 28 May 2020

Le Soir, 23-24 May 2020

DG ITEC Newsletter, October 2020

Le Soir 29 October 2020

Le Soir 3 November 2020

Le Soir 6 November 2020

MEETINGS, EXCHANGES OF VIEW AND SEMINARS

Several meetings with the Secretary General, K. Welle

3-4 Oct 2019: EP Bureau Away Days, (Bazoches, France)

17 Oct 2019: MEP Vice-president Dobrev and ICT Working Group

21 Oct 2019: EP Management Team: short presentation

21 Oct 2019: Staff Committee: debate on "EPA Working Methods"

22 Oct 2019: F. Debié EPRS and L. Délepine CSG

12 Nov 2019: MEP Vice-president Kolaja

25 Nov 2019: C. Neto PERS

03 Dec 2019: Seminar on Artificial Intelligence

05 Dec 2019: Seminar on "EPA Working Methods" (Luxembourg)

09 Dec 2019: Conference on "EPA Working Methods" (University of Milan)

06 Jan 2020: F. Miatto (Cabinet of the President)

08 Jan 2020: EPRS Book Talk on "EPA Working Methods" (Brussels)

10 Jan 2020: EPA Management Innovation Day (Brussels)

15 Jan 2020: S. Sabbioni DPO

15 Jan 2020: P. Paridans ITEC

22 Jan 2020: Max Planck Lecture on "EPA Working Methods" (Luxembourg)

29 Jan 2020: W. Petrucci ITEC

29 Jan 2020: EPRS/STOA, The Future of Artificial Intelligence for Europe

7 February 2020: M. Maciejewski IPOL

10 February 2020: EP Management Team

11 February 2020: ITEC Management Meeting

13 February 2020: S. Eilertsen, ITEC

14 February 2020: Prof. G. Sgueo, New York University, Florence, & EPRS

25 February 2020: C. Neto PERS, P. Sabbatucci and P. Paridans ITEC

25 February 2020: Prof. A. Donati, Max Planck Institute and Nancy University

25 February 2020: Prof. E. Francesconi, President of the International Association for AI

5 March 2020: S. Mameli ITEC

13 March 2020: S. Sabbioni DPO (online)

9-10 April 2020: L. Délepine CSG (online)

29-30 April: M.J. Martinez Iglesias, Legal Service

11 September 2020: EPA Management Innovation Day (Brussels)

14 to 17 September: International Democracy Week (online)

24-25 September 2020: EP Bureau Away Days (Brussels)

9 and 11 November 2020: V. Köykkä ITEC

In addition to Secretary General Klaus Welle, I would like to thank from the bottom of my heart all the people whose names appear on the above list: their contribution was truly of great importance in enriching and improving the text. In addition, I should like to add a special word of thanks to Carmela Toscano, Sandra Angelini and Gabriele Babini, who have constantly accompanied me throughout the study and editing of the report: their contribution by way of organisational and secretarial work, as well as in researching the documents and looking over the contents has been invaluable. Lastly, special thanks goes to my friend and colleague Robert Bray, who has revised my English from top to bottom: it goes without saying, however, that the responsibility for any remaining errors is mine and mine alone.

Photo Credits

www.ingramcontent.com/pod-product-compliance
Ingram Content Group UK Ltd.
Pitfield, Milton Keynes, MK11 3LW, UK
UKHW022029190726
13853UKWH00005B/2176